POST-MERGER INTEGRATION

Improving
Shareholders'
Values After
A Merger

Published in 2010 by
Corporate Turnaround Centre Pte Ltd.

Printed in Singapore
by Mentor Media Printing Pte Ltd

9 8 7 6 5 4 3 2 1
09 10

INTEGRATION AND PRESERVING
SHAREHOLDER VALUE

Background of ErDr Mike Teng

Dr Teng is widely recognized as a turnaround CEO in Asia by the news media. He has been interviewed on the international media on many occasions on the subject of corporate turnaround and transformation as well as internet marketing such as the Malaysian Business Radio, BFM 89-9, News Radio FM 93.8, Malaysian Business Radio, Edge Radio (USA), the Channel News Asia, the Boss Magazine, Economic Bulletin, the Today, World Executive Digest, Lianhe ZaoPao, StarBiz and the Straits Times. His online seminars are broadcasted globally by Success University and SkyquestCom to 120 countries.

Dr Mike Teng is the author of a best-selling book *"Corporate Turnaround: Nursing a sick company back to health"*, in 2002 which is also translated into the Bahasa Indonesia and Mandarin. His book is endorsed by management guru Professor Philip Kotler and business tycoons Mr Oei Hong Leong and Dr YY Wong. He subsequently authored more than fifteen management books.

He has authored two books on merger and acquisition, namely *Fundamentals of Buying and Selling of Companies* and *Buying and Selling of Distressed Companies*. He also trained merchant bankers and advised private equity in merger and acquisition. Dr Teng has personally went through many merger and acquisition situations.

Dr Teng is currently the Managing Director of Corporate Turnaround Centre Pte Ltd (www.corporateturnaroundcentre.com) which provides corporate training and management advisory services in the region. He is the national trainer appointed by the National University of Singapore to train displaced senior managers and deploy them to run SMEs under the NUS/SPRING/SBF Business Advisory Program.

He has more than 29 years of experience in starting new plants, strategic planning, operational management responsibilities in the Asia Pacific region, primarily in the manufacturing industry. Of these, he held Chief Executive Officer's positions for 19 years in multi-national and publicly listed companies. He was the CEO of a US MNC based in Singapore for ten years. He also advised several boards of directors of publicly-listed companies.

Dr Teng served as the Executive Council member for fourteen years and the last four years as the President of the Marketing Institute of Singapore (2000 – 2004), the national marketing association.

Dr Teng holds a Doctor in Business Administration (DBA) from the University of South Australia, Master in Business Administration (MBA) and Bachelor in Mechanical Engineering (BEng) from the National University of Singapore. He is also a Professional Engineer (P Eng, Singapore), Chartered Engineer (C Eng, UK) and Fellow Member of several prestigious professional institutes namely, Chartered Institute of Marketing (FCIM), Chartered Management Institute (FCMI), Institute of Mechanical Engineers (FIMechE), Marketing Institute of Singapore (FMIS), Institute of Electrical Engineers (FIEE) and Senior Member of Singapore Computer Society (SMSCS). He is also a Practising Management Consultant (PMC) certified by the Singapore government.

Introduction

In the last few decades, the world has witnessed the phenomenon of corporations voluntarily combining with other existing enterprises to tap an ever-growing and widening market base. The world also witnessed hostile takeovers – acquisitions done by entities that wished to cash in on the success and the resources of established corporations.

Mergers had often been preceded by a lot of hype, raising shareholders expectations. Yet, the results of many of such mergers or acquisitions have been disappointing. Only about 30 to 50% of mergers or acquisitions have been reported to be successful in increasing value.

What happened to all the expected benefits touted by merger sponsors?

In many instances, post-merger integration issues, mostly cultural differences, were pointed out as a major factor in determining the success or failure of a merger.

This e-book aims to examine post-merger integration issues that can make or break a merger. Note that the perspective adopted in this e-book is that of the acquiring corporation or the buyer.

PART I

MERGERS AND ACQUISITIONS DEFINED[ii]

A merger is the combination of two or more companies (called constituent corporations) to create a larger company. It is a tool by which corporations expand operations with the ultimate aim of increasing profits. In some cases, both corporations may be dissolved, in which case a new, combined corporation with a different name, usually a combination of the merging corporation's original names, emerges. In other cases, a corporation may be absorbed and only the surviving corporation retains its name.

A merger is distinguished from an acquisition wherein a person or entity simply acquires controlling interest in an existing corporation. An acquisition may or may not result in a combination of the resources of two or more companies since the acquiring shareholder may opt to maintain the acquired corporation as a separate or independent entity. However, when the acquired company's operations are integrated into the operations of the acquiring corporation, a combination becomes effective and a larger company is created.

A merger is often voluntary and friendly in the sense that the governing boards of the merging corporations reach an agreement to combine the resources of their companies. In some cases, they may be "forced" by a country's economic or financial policies. For instance, a country facing a crisis in the banking sector may require banks to raise capital and reserve requirements as a condition for the renewal of their licenses. This in turn may force small banks to merge together so that their combined resources meet the new capital and reserve requirements, enabling them to continue operating as banking institutions.

An acquisition sometimes may not be voluntary in nature; in the sense that an individual or entity may buy up a corporation's stocks in the open market in order to gain controlling interest against the wishes of the target corporation's board.

This is what is known as a hostile takeover and this is what the public may be most familiar with since it very often involves a target corporation's individual stockholders and creates interesting public corporate drama. This in turn makes it a likely subject for a lot for movies and novels.

A merger or acquisition can be seen as a way by which a company may achieve growth in terms of size, market share, productivity, etc. This is in contrast to organic growth which is achieved when a company develops its own market or resources without resorting to the acquisition process.[iii]

TYPES OF MERGERS AND REASONS FOR MERGERS[iv]

SYNERGY

As stated earlier, some mergers occur as a result of government policy or as a survival response – "merge or be dissolved." In most cases however, the motive goes beyond survival. It is to increase profit because of perceived "synergy" – or the potential ability of individual organizations or groups to be more successful or productive as a result of a merger.

The synergy may result from the combined firm's ability to exploit economies of scale (savings achieved in the cost of production because the initial investment can be defrayed across a greater number of producing units); the elimination of duplicated functions; the sharing of managerial expertise; acquisition of new technology; and the ability to raise larger amounts of capital.

MARKET POWER

A desire for greater market power could also be a reason for a merger – resulting in "horizontal mergers" – the combination of corporations with similar product lines such as, when two manufacturers of luxury cars merge to become a bigger manufacturer of luxury cars.

If both corporations have separate markets, as in the case of a merger between a car manufacturer based in Europe and a car manufacturer based in the USA, the merger could also be classified as a "market extension merger."

CONTROL OVER MANUFACTURING AND MARKETING PROCESSES

On the other hand, a desire to have more control over the manufacturing or selling process within a single industry may result in a "vertical merger" – the combination of firms involved in the same business but at different levels It is possible for one of the combining firms to have been a supplier. For instance, a soft drinks company merges with a bottling corporation that supplies it with containers for its soft drinks products.

DIVERSIFICATION

Diversification may be a motive for merging two corporations. For instance; two interrelated firms not in the same line of business may enter into a "congeneric merger." Scholars cite Prudential Financial's acquisition of Bache Halsey Stuart Shields Incorporated. Prudential was mainly into insurance services while Bache was engaged in stock brokerage and investment banking services. Both were in the financial services industry but were not engaged in the same activities.

This kind of merger may also be called a *"product extension merger"* which, by definition, is a merger that takes place between two companies dealing in products that are related to each other and operate in the same market.

A product extension merger allows the merging companies to group together their products and get access to a bigger set of consumers. It also increases likelihood of the merged corporation to earn higher profits.

Mergers between corporations operating in unrelated industries are called *"conglomerate mergers."* For instance, a food manufacturing giant merging with a corporation supplying electric power is said to be in a "conglomerate merger." The desire of building an empire has been cited as a motive for engaging in such acquisitions which, in most cases, do not create synergies.

REVERSE MERGER

A reverse merger is a method by which a private company (not listed in a stock exchange) can become a publicly traded company without the expense and time requirements involved in an initial public offering (IPO). In some jurisdictions, this is referred to as "back-door listing." The target company is usually a dormant or shell company.

TRIANGULAR OR SUBSIDIARY MERGER

A triangular or subsidiary merger occurs when a corporation wishes to acquire a target corporation without necessarily becoming a constituent corporation. The acquiring corporation forms a subsidiary or uses an existing one to morgo with the target corporation so that the target corporation becomes a subsidiary of the acquiring corporation.

GLOBALIZATION

According to current studies, there are two main factors driving cross-border merger and acquisition activities namely, *environment* factors and *strategic* factors. The motivations for M&A's reported by the leading global companies are generally classified into six categories:
- Degree of oligopoly within an industry
- Excess production capacity
- De-regulation
- Customer-relation
- Separation of production and product design
- R&D investment [v]

Oligopoly has been defined as a market in which control over the supply of a commodity is in the hands of a small number of producers and each one can influence prices and affect competitors. [vi] Recent studies show that merger and acquisition activities in oil, steel, automobile, telecommunications were triggered by a high degree of oligopoly. An example given was that when BP and Amoco merged, Exxon took over Mobil to become the largest oil company in the industry. On the other hand, the lack of an excess capacity did not seem to directly prompt the formation of mergers and acquisitions. Companies resolved the problem of capacity by moving their production facilities to other countries or by outsourcing. Deregulation in industries such as in the banking, oil, steel, pharmaceutical and telecommunications industries, however, was a major factor in bringing about mergers and acquisitions. Studies also showed that there was more merger and acquisition activity in industries where the output possessed the characteristic of a service and involved developing customer relations such as banking and telecommunications. Functional specialization and the cost of research and development, on the other hand, led to less merger or acquisitions or did not have much impact on mergers and acquisitions. [vii]

To sum up, leading global companies used mergers and acquisitions as a means of achieving growth, oligopoly, and globalization. They took mergers and acquisitions as a means of rapid growth with three strategic goals:
  • enjoy first mover advantage in rapidly growing markets,
  • reduce uncertainty in R&D investment, and
  • obtain knowledge, human resources, know-how, and experience that cannot be easily realized through strategic alliances or foreign direct investment.

There is, however, evidence that Asian companies still seem to prefer organic growth to inorganic growth using mergers and acquisitions. [viii]

STAGES OF A MERGER OR ACQUISITION

In the legal world, a merger usually goes through the following stages:
1) Proposing a merger to the governing boards of the constituent corporations and obtaining their approval;
2) Informing shareholders of the constituent corporations about the proposed merger and obtaining shareholder approval;
3) Conducting a legal due diligence;
4) Preparing and filing documents such as the Articles of Merger;
5) Complying with regulatory requirements and obtaining approval of the merger from applicable state or government agencies.

In the business world, the merger's stages could be classified as
(1) The planning stage;
(2) The acquisition stage; and
(3) The execution and post-merger integration stage.

The legal process would fall under the Acquisition Stage although there could be overlapping with the planning and post-merger integration stages.

THE PLANNING STAGE[ix]

The planning stage would include:

(1) Identifying and assigning key people to take charge or facilitate the various stages of the merger process;

(2) Identifying the vision of the corporation and its reasons and goals for entering into a merger;

(3) Based on item number two, seeking and identifying the target corporation which may involve seeking corporations that had placed themselves up for sale;

(4) Conducting studies and investigations such as an industry study to determine the feasibility of a merger, a financial study to determine the potential value of the target corporation, management practices study to see if target corporations would fit into its structure, a study of the costs of the merger and the length of time it would take to carry out such a merger;

(5) Based on the results of items one to three, determining the legal structure of the combined companies, whether a new corporation should be created to absorb the constituent corporations or whether the target corporation could simply be absorbed;

(6) Preparing a proposal or a bid (a letter of intent) to be sent to a target corporation.

ACQUISITION STAGE[x]

Should a target corporation respond favorably to a merger offer, the acquiring corporation then proceeds to conduct due diligence on both the financial and legal risks of the target corporation since corporate liabilities are absorbed by the merged entities.

Due diligence is a process by which an acquiring company investigates various aspects of the corporation – normally those that pertain to the financial and legal risks of a corporation. It is a process wherein an acquirer studies the object of its desire (i.e., the target company), a process or tool to gather more information and to assess the realistic values of a target company by evaluating its strengths, weaknesses, risks, synergies, and the overall fit within the acquirer's strategy. Due diligence can cover financial, tax, commercial, operational, human resource, management, pension, information technology, legal, intellectual property, anti-trust, compliance and insurance/risk management due diligence. [xi]

FINANCIAL DUE DILIGENCE[xii]

For the financial due diligence aspect of the merger process,, an acquiring corporation usually hires accountants and financial consultants to focus on financial analysis and examine the accuracy of financial statements,, look for potential tax exposures and other financial liabilities and make an assessment of internal controls to determine whether opportunities exist to lessen tax liabilities not previously used by the existing management.

Financial due diligence enables the acquiring company to become familiar with the accounting practices of the target corporation so that the incoming management may plan for consolidation of this function after the merger which could result in reducing the duplication of efforts and overhead expenses.

LEGAL DUE DILIGENCE[xiii]

Lawyers, on the other hand, are hired to examine the legal affairs of the target company to look for legal risks. They scrutinize all contracts and agreements entered into by the company such as lease contracts, employment contracts, contracts with suppliers', IT contracts and technology or service contracts among others.

Lawyers also examine company records to determine whether the target company had complied with requirements of various government agencies, when applicable as in the case of regulated industries.

They examine litigation matters that the company is involved with or likely to get involved with.

In other words, lawyers look at the legal implications of the target company's dealings with government agencies, suppliers, employees, consultants, service providers and the like. These relationships are a source of obligations – current or future – that could have an impact on the merged firm's future operations.

OTHER DUE DILIGENCE

Other due diligence that may be conducted would be an inspection of the target company's facilities and capital equipment. This would serve several purposes: to help assess the possibility of using current facilities and equipment together with the existing facilities of the acquiring corporation, to assess the costs of upgrading or introducing improvements to the facilities and the capital equipment and lastly to assess the value of the target corporation's assets.

An emerging practice among corporations is to include a "cultural due diligence" as part of the overall due-diligence process. Before and after issuing the Letter of Intent and certainly before the deal is closed; due-diligence activities can and should include assessments of the historical and present labour/management culture and of critical human resource policies and procedures making up what employees view as core cultural elements. [xiv]

Some consultants suggest that due diligence should be extended to all issues of business and strategy to answer the question "What can both-the acquiring and the targeted company offer to customers?"

To answer that question, due diligence would cover areas that are not subject to traditional due diligence such as:
- Customers
- Competencies and abilities of staff
- Competitors
- Costs
- Culture[xv]

This type of due diligence would be useful in creating the post-merger integration plan and in identifying, valuing and maximizing expected synergies and is, in fact, recommended in order to ensure merger success.

NEGOTIATIONS/STRUCTURING THE DEAL

After the due diligence, acquiring corporations are in a better bargaining position to adjust the new bid based on the intrinsic value and the value of the perceived synergies.

A number of consultants suggest that in their eagerness to acquire a corporation for its perceived synergies, buyers often pay substantial premiums, as much as 40% more than the stock market valuations.

Before making a new bid, consultants suggest that buyers determine the target corporation's value using the following techniques

- asset valuation
- historical earnings valuation,
- discounted cash flow (DCF) valuation
- future maintainable earnings valuation
- relative valuation (comparable company & comparable transactions)[xvi]

ASSET VALUATION

Asset valuation has been defined as the process of determining the current worth of a company through the value of capital assets or fixed assets at which they should be shown in the target company's balance sheet.

Capital assets are fixed assets employed as a means of generating income, generally the one on which depreciation is claimed. Fixed assets, on the other hand, refer to land, buildings, equipment, machinery, vehicles, leasehold improvements, and other such items. Any asset expected to last, or be in use for more than one year is considered as a fixed asset.

This valuation method is usually used if the target company is not profitable and is set for liquidation. It is also the method that lenders and banks tend to favor. Experts say, however, that this method does not reflect the total value of the corporation and does not take into account Intangibles such as goodwill. Matters such as a loyal customer base and a solid relationship with suppliers could form part of goodwill and are not considered when making a valuation of the corporation. [xvii]

HISTORICAL EARNINGS VALUATION

A method of valuation is based on the target corporation's historical earnings. In contrast with the Asset Valuation method, it allows a goodwill value over and above the market value of the assets if justified by the earnings. It is said that this method is seen as the most relevant of all valuation approaches for buyers or for acquirers. It tells them what the target company has historically provided to its owners in terms of cash. The assumption is that the past earnings can predict future performance. Experts take financial data from the company's previous three to five years in drawing its conclusions.[xviii]

DISCOUNTED CASH FLOW VALUATION (DCF)

This approach focuses on estimates of future streams of cash flow which are then discounted to a "present value" or what they would be worth today.

It is a method that requires parties to agree on which future cash streams to use and for how long (for instance, it could take into account obsolescence of a product or technology); an estimate of the revenue stream (how much income will be generated in the future); and the rate of discount of this stream of cash flow to arrive at its present value.

This method recognizes factors such as industry reputation, popularity with customers and other "goodwill" factors in its assessment of company value.

According to some consultants, the discounted cash flow method is usually used to value new or immature businesses or a business in which there is considerable variation in income or expenditure expectations. [xix]

FUTURE MAINTAINABLE EARNINGS VALUATION OR CAPITALIZATION OF MAINTAINABLE EARNINGS

According to the Accounting Glossary of Ventureline,, future maintainable earnings valuation or capitalization of maintainable earnings is a valuation method that involves capitalizing the future maintainable earnings by the application of a suitably chosen capitalization rate or multiple. Earnings may refer to profit after tax ("PAT") or earnings before interest and tax ("EBIT"). [xx]

This methodology is a variation of the discounted cash flow method and requires consideration of several factors such as an estimate of future maintainable earnings having regard to historical operating results and forecasts of future earnings; a determination of an appropriate capitalization rate which will reflect the risks inherent in the business including sensitivity to industry risk factors, growth prospects, the general economic outlook and alternative investment opportunities; and a separate assessment of any surplus or unrelated assets and liabilities which are not essential to the continuing earning capacity of the business operations.[xxi]

The formula for calculating the value of a business is:

Future Maintainable Earnings X Capitalization Factor = Value of Business.

The capitalization factor is defined as: "any multiple or divisor used to convert anticipated economic benefits of a single period into value." [xxii]

Experts have said that the capitalization of future maintainable earnings method is the most common way of valuing an existing business in good order, as it usually aligns reasonably well with the expectations of potential purchasers. [xxiii]

RELATIVE VALUATION (COMPARABLE COMPANY & COMPARABLE TRANSACTIONS)

As it's label states, this approach looks at companies which are comparable to the target company in terms of industry, size, growth rates, capitalization and other factors. These comparable companies would have a market value that is known or observable such as a publicly traded company to establish a value for the company under examination. [xxiv]

Experts have stated that this approach is inherently flawed since it is rare that two businesses are truly comparable. However, businesses in the same industry would have some characteristics in common and a careful comparison may allow a conclusion to be drawn about a range of value. [xxv]

NEGOTIATIONS AND CLOSING THE DEAL[xxvi]

At this point, the acquiring corporation and the target company may enter into negotiations regarding the terms and conditions of the merger and acquisition.

By this time, negotiators would have determined the corporate structure. For instance it could be a merger where the target corporation is absorbed and the acquiring corporation survives. Or it could be a consolidation of the corporations so that both corporations are dissolved and the two corporations are combined into a single but larger corporation.

A purchase price would have been suggested and reviewed. However, aside from the purchase price, negotiators discuss details such as the timing and the form of payment (cash or stock swap); exclusions and inclusions in the sale (if it is an acquisition); transfer of properties/ equipment; personnel policies—retention, retirement of employees, transfer of personnel, pension funds,; schedule of the merger/acquisition, transition periods, etc.

Negotiators may also, at this point, pinpoint key personnel to handle the integration phase or assign a consulting firm to handle the integration phase of the corporation and agree upon a transition plan to address issues such as shakeups in executive management, ownership structure, incentives, shareholder exit strategies, equity holding periods, strategy, market presence, training, make up of sales force, administration, accounting and production.

These details are set forth in a Merger Agreement or Articles of Merger or a similar type of document which are then presented to the merging corporations' respective boards and stockholders.

Once the necessary approvals are obtained, the merger plan is submitted to the appropriate government agencies for approval.

As stated earlier, payment may be made either in cash or in stock. In outright acquisitions, cash (or a combination of cash and debt) is paid to stockholders directly or through the stock market. In mergers, a stock swap may be resorted to wherein shareholders of the target corporation end up being shareholders of the merged corporation. Payments may also be made partly in cash or partly in stock.

PART II

POST-MERGER INTEGRATION

Once the necessary government approvals are obtained, the merger may be deemed to have been completed. However, the "end" of the merger process is actually just the formal beginning of the integration process.

Corporate news since the 1980's suggest at least 50% of mergers undertaken were disappointments. Some highly publicized mergers (think AOL and Time Warner and Daimler Chrysler) eventually were "demerged." Yet, despite such highly publicized failed mergers; corporations still push through with the strategy of mergers and acquisitions.

As observed by Asian scholars, mergers and acquisitions are attractive as they create synergies and economies of scale by expanding operations and markets and contributing to eliminating inefficiencies and increasing productivity and profitability. They are also powerful and pervasive creating other intended and unintended effects at the macro and micro levels. Large mergers and acquisitions may affect the entire economy. They may lead to significant changes in the structure of employment, employee earnings and investor behavior. [xxvii]

Given the impact of mergers and acquisitions, it is in the interest of the merger participants (both the acquiring and the target companies) as well as that of society at large, to find out what factors contribute to merger success.

WHAT MAKES MERGERS SUCCESSFUL?

According to consultants Albert J. Viscio, John R. Harbison, Amy Asin and Richard P. Vitaro, the most successful companies link effective strategic formulation, pre-merger planning and post-merger integration. They assert that having all three components is critical for success:

- A vision, strategically formulated, for where the company is going and how the deal fits. Companies identify the appropriate targets and get the deal done.
- A pre-merger process that targets companies with the right capabilities gets the deal done and begins the integration through rigorous planning and building of trust among the players.
- A post-merger process that seeks to capture well-defined sources of value and is led in a way that captures as much value as possible as quickly as possible. [xxviii]

One author states that one way of assuring post-merger success is finding the right company to marry. He likens a merger to a marriage; stating that if a poor choice of partner in marriage leads to conflict, unhappiness and often divorce; in the same manner, a careless selection of a partner for a merger, acquisition, or joint venture dooms the chances for a successful integration of companies. [xxix]

The same author also emphasizes talent (or know-how) in acquiring and integrating corporations as a key to post merger success. He states that if the company has no talent for acquiring and integrating companies, acquisitions and integration should be a strategy for last resort. And if it has a talent for acquisitions and integration, it should ask itself, what can it bring to the target corporation? Is it good at acquiring similar or dissimilar companies? It is his thesis that if you don't have a track record for acquiring corporations, then don't even attempt to go into a merger. Neither does he think it advisable to go into a merger for purely financial reasons or as an "escape hatch" as it leads to a lack of business focus. And he states that forward or backward integration (acquiring the company of customers or suppliers) would be advisable only if it would solve a size problem. Buying in order to assure supply or to capture a market often does not work. He also recommends that the integration approach be tailored. [xxx]

Another author states that research shows that there are actions that can improve the probability of acquisition success:

- The target firm's assets are complementary to the acquirer's assets because with complementary assets integrating two firms' operations has a higher probability of creating synergy and frequently produces unique capabilities and core competencies. The

14

acquiring firm can maintain its focus on core businesses while leveraging the complementary assets and capabilities of the acquired firm.

- Friendly acquisitions facilitate integration of the firms involved because firms work together to find ways to integrate their operations to create synergy as contrasted with hostile takeovers where animosity frequently results between the two top management teams which in turn affect working relationships in the newly created firm. More key personnel in the acquired firm may be lost, and those who remain may resist the changes necessary to integrate the two firms. The premium paid is also lower because the deal is friendly.

- Effective due diligence processes – involving the deliberate and careful selection of target firms and an evaluation of the relative health of those firms –so that the firm with strongest complements is acquired and overpayment is avoided.
- Financial slack in both the acquiring and acquired firms also has frequently contributed to success in acquisitions as it provides access to financing for the acquisitions. If debt is used to finance the acquisition, firms with successful acquisitions reduce the debt quickly, partially by selling off assets from the acquired firm, especially non-complimentary or poorly performing assets. By doing so, they maintain a moderate level of debt after the acquisition and keep debt costs low.
- Long term investments such as significant and continuous investments in R&D activities show a strong managerial commitment to innovation; a characteristic that is increasingly important to continuing competitiveness.
- Flexibility and adaptability are essential to successful acquisitions-- executives of both the acquiring firm and the target firm with experience in managing change and learning from acquisitions will be more skilled at adapting their capabilities to new environments and will be more adept at integrating the two organizations which is particularly important since no two firms have exactly synonymous organizational cultures. [xxxi]

One consultant succinctly sums up the three inter-related activities which form the defining elements of successful acquisitions as follows:
- buying the right company;
- paying the right amount;
- and then capturing whatever value is needed to overcome any premium that was paid.

The first is a matter of strategy, the second is (for the most part) one of technical analysis and due diligence, and the third -- the Post Merger Integration -- is both an art and a science. A failure of any one is likely to result in a destruction of shareholder value. [xxxii]

IMPORTANCE OF POST MERGER INTEGRATION

The importance of post-merger integration is derived from the fact that value creation can only begin when the organizations begin to work towards the purpose of the acquisition. In other words, integration is the source of value creation. [xxxiii]

Also, mergers and acquisitions are said to have a success rate of only about 25% to 50% at best and post-merger integration is often blamed as the major reason why mergers and acquisition deals are less successful than they should be. [xxxiv]

In almost all commentaries or studies on the subject matter, PMI has been pointed out as an important key to merger success. One author states that it may be the one major cause of failure in cross-border mergers. [xxxv]

The same author states that studies show that cultural fit has a major effect on post-merger performance and that companies that allow multi-culturalism and prevent too much control perform better than less permissive firms [xxxvi] and that the origin of competitive advantage is the "local environment". Thus, if a German firm is interested in the computer software industry, it might want to acquire a firm in the best local environment (i.e., Silicon Valley) and try to help its expertise spread to the parent firm. [xxxvii]

INTEGRATION DEFINED

So what is PMI?

Integration has been defined as the act of combining into an integral whole- a consolidation of two corporations. Post-merger integration or PMI refers to the aspect of an organizational merger that involves combining the original socio-technical systems of the merging organizations into one such newly-combined system or the process of combining two or more organizations into a single organization which involves several organizational systems, such as people, resources and tasks.[xxxviii]

Post-merger integration has also been defined as "a gradual and interactive process, in which the individuals from two or more organisations learn to co-operate in the transfer of strategic capabilities." [xxxix]

For this e-book, Post Merger Integration will refer to the process of harmonizing organizational elements between merging corporations in order to make the merger work so that it achieves the envisioned goals and aims of the corporate combination.

The definition of PMI success, on the other hand, is not based on share prices but on the extent to which targets like cost synergies, cross selling or know-how transfer were met and includes criteria such as implementation efficiency and social compatibility as seen in the company's management systems, its underlying ideology, and in its relationship with employees. (for example, employee participation, working hours, pay, health and social security benefits etc). [xl]

LEVELS OR DIMENSIONS OF INTEGRATION

Analysts state that integration takes place on several levels or dimensions [xli] with one author classifying them as procedural, physical and socio-cultural integration. [xlii]

Procedural integration refers to the process of combining systems and procedures of the merged companies at the operating, management control, and strategic planning levels. The objective of such integration is to homogenize and standardize work procedures. Physical integration of resources and assets usually accompanies procedural integration. Managerial and socio-cultural integration involves a complex combination of issues related to the selection or transfer of leaders, changes in organizational structure, development of a consistent culture and the increases in the commitment and motivation of personnel. [xliii]

Other analysts state that merger success is a function dealing with task integration and human integration. Task integration is defined as the identification and realization of operational synergies measured in terms of transferred capabilities and resource sharing. Human integration is concerned primarily with generating satisfaction and ultimately a shared identity among the employees from the combining organizations. [xliv]

One author cites the four degrees of integration:
- Total autonomy,
- Restructuring followed by financial controls,
- Integration of main systems and
- Full integration. [xlv]

In relation to the four degrees of integration, one author asserts that Integration need not be total and cites five different PMI approaches:

- **Preservation or stand-alone:** Both companies are kept separate with almost no or only minimal changes. The complete opposite of integration, is, in the author's opinion, a very good choice in order not to destroy the value of a transaction.
- **Confederation**: Companies enjoy a relatively high level of autonomy, but a variety of interdependencies and some control.
- **Absorption**: One company is fully integrated into the other company or adopts its standards, processes, etc.
- **Best of both worlds** or **best of class:** Both companies create a combined entity taking over superior parts from both, or introducing best-of-class standards.
- **Transformation:** whereby the integrated companies try to create something entirely new ranging from a giant leap in terms of geographic or product coverage to even a fundamental change in the business model, for example. [xlvi]

HOLISTIC APPROACH IN POST MERGER INTEGRATION

In general, literature on the subject of PMI speaks about the necessity to adopt a holistic approach.

One author states that PMI should be put in the driver's seat of the merger and acquisition process as an important step that goes along the complete M&A process from beginning to end. He asserts that if you position PMI as a simple step after such tasks as strategy development, target search, due diligence, negotiations and closing for a limited time period only, you tend to absolutely underestimate the contribution and the difference that PMI makes in making deals valuable. [xlvii]

Two consultants state that in their experience, when mergers and acquisitions do work, the integration process seems to be holistic, fluid and well executed. [xlviii]
Another author states that the post-merger phase is linked to the larger overall acquisition process and its specific objectives. It is not an independent activity. [xlix]

A merger consultant states that there is a need to move away from the idea that M&A and PMI are two separate and totally distinct activities. In fact, he states that the very name "post merger integration" is problematic because it leaves the impression that all the preparation for the integration should wait until after the deal is done and that other critical elements of deal success, such as estimating the complexity and cost of the integration, the alterability of synergies, and the organization implications of the merged company, should be addressed only after closing. He points out that the probability of deal success goes up considerably when the key elements of PMI are not only started before closing, but when the likely risks and challenges of the integration are considered *at the very beginning* of the M&A process -- when the acquirer is deciding what to buy and what to pay. [i]

He goes on to state that "all of the elements that affect PMI success, especially the culture of the companies, must be assessed and rolled into the synergy value (and price to pay) calculation. In essence, there should not be a separate M&A and PMI process, but a fully holistic approach to the deal, from strategy to target identification to valuation to integration. This involves looking 'downstream' at business core processes and the nuts and bolts of how things work, and in getting the people who know how to design and implement changes to these systems and processes involved up front, especially during the valuation stage." [ii]

Ronald N. Ashkenas, Lawrence J. DeMonaco, and Suzanne C. Francis—consultants for GE Capital, a corporation that had become an expert in growing through acquisitions—state that "acquisition integration is not a discrete phase of a deal and does not begin when the documents are signed. Rather, it is a process that begins with due diligence and runs through the ongoing management of the new enterprise." In their experience, they discovered that thinking about integration as early as the due diligence phase could speed the eventual melding. They also found that **being** sensitive to integration issues during the due diligence phase began to foster better decisions about whether to proceed with an acquisition at all. [iii]

PMI SHOULD BE TAILORED

Aside from a holistic approach, the authors point out that integrations are more likely to be successful if they are tailored. As stated by one author, one standard approach does not get the job done. It is true that there are common elements to examine in acquisitions and mergers. For instance, it is obvious that the organizations, strategies and operating systems of combining companies must be made to fit. However, there are individual elements, the importance of which would depend on the specific merger candidate. The author emphasizes that you need to tailor your integration approach in a number of disparate key factors to succeed. The failure to do the tailoring, in large part, explains why there are so many firms that are combined but not truly integrated. [liii]

This view is echoed by a consultant who says that the reality is that while there are many common elements to integration execution (and common pitfalls to avoid) each deal has its own complexities and idiosyncrasies. He cites differences in the timing needed to achieve synergies, cost or revenue based synergies, delays due to regulatory approval, and the degree of overlapping in geography and business practices. He suggests that instead of using a 'one size fits all approach,' the integration process should be customized to the specific transaction. The new best practice is to have an organized and logical approach which includes all of the necessary steps and activities but which is flexible enough to match up to the unique requirements of the deal. The approach should be modified to fit the deal, rather than the deal being forced into the approach. [liv]

Kummer suggests that the strategy can determine the kind of integration approach that the acquirer might want to follow. For instance, if a corporation enters into a merger with another company to generate additional growth by selling existing products in an existing market, it could acquire competitors. Therefore, the company would rather aim for solid consolidation and high synergy realization and would do best choosing the absorption or bets of both world's approach of PMI.[lv]

If a corporation desires a combination of existing and new like product development or market development where the company pursues a medium risk growth strategy to stimulate growth by either selling its existing products to new customers in new geographical markets or distribution channels or tries to introduce new products to existing clients or in its current markets, it may achieve its goal through acquisitions. Kummer suggests that a company might rather go for the confederation approach for its PMI. When going for a more risky strategy of diversification (both new, lower right corner) then clearly a preservation might be more preferable.[lvi]

Consultants Booz, Allen & Hamilton posit t that a vision for value creation is crucial to the integration process. It enables integration leaders to ask the following questions:
- How will we create value?
- What must we do to realize the potential of this deal?
- What do we redesign, create, adopt or eliminate? (By segment, organization, process or geography?)
- What do we need to compete as an institution?
- What must be integrated immediately? What can wait?

By answering those questions, the team can proceed to the next question – what approach should we take? Do we absorb, create or attach, etc. [lvii]

Another writer states that there are three things to look at in shaping an approach to integration; company size, company nationality, and company organizational structure. [lviii]
Merging a large and small company or two drastically different size contracting companies should be approached differently from merging two large sized firms. The difference would be in terms of complexity -- the number of executives involved, dynamics of management, etc. [lix]

With respect to company nationality, he states that to achieve success, one must be cognizant and take into account that differences in attitudes, history, social security policies, incentive systems and culture exist. For example, he states that when you merge an American company with a French one, it is important to realize that the French do not reveal or speak openly about their remuneration levels. It is considered in poor taste. Even the salary of the most senior executives is not revealed in public documents. This means, for example, that performance-based compensation, as understood in an American context, does not work in most European settings. [lx]

As for company organization, the same author asserts that an acquiring company's specific organization structure always strongly influences the type of post-merger integration approach that is required. For instance, he cites the example of a corporation that relies heavily on outsourcing. If it wanted to merge with a company that relies heavily on the use of in-house resources, the integration process will require extensive structural and behavioral modifications of staff to achieve harmony. He states that what actions to take to do the right mix would need to be addressed in the post-merger integration plan.[lxi]

LEADING AND MANAGING INTEGRATION

Acquisition experts Ashkenas, DeMonaco, and Francis state that one of the lessons learned by GE Capital in its years of using acquisition as its growth strategy is that integration management is a full-time job that needs to be recognized as a distinct business function, just like operations, marketing or finance. They state that in the GE Capital experience, it took many years for them to answer the questions -- who should focus on integration and who is the one person responsible for making sure that the new company becomes a fully functioning, high-performing part of the acquirer.[lxii]

The due diligence team with its knowledge about the acquired company and its insight into what would be needed to integrate it usually disbanded after the deal was struck. Functional and business leaders of the acquiring GE company typically focused only on the integration of their particular units. Newly acquired business leaders did not have sufficient knowledge of GE Capital, its resources, or its integration requirements and tended to be preoccupied with running the company as well as dealing with personal issues (for instance: protecting, reassuring or out placing their people; figuring out whether they wanted to stay in the new company and proving that their company was even better than what the buyers thought.)[lxiii]

The business leader of the acquiring GE business was usually assumed to be accountable for integration. That, however, was an unrealistic assignment since he usually had other units to run and was not dedicated fully to the new acquisition. And even when he could devote time to the acquisition, his focus was not on integration of cultures, processes, and people but on business issues such as profit growth, staffing key jobs, and customer retention. His position of authority also often limited his ability to facilitate integration since people in a newly acquired company need someone they can talk to freely,, ask "stupid" questions and find out how things work at GE Capital. They needed a guide to the new culture and a bridge between their company and GE Capital. The last person who fitted that role was the new boss they wanted to impress. [lxiv]

By chance and necessity, the role of designated integration manager evolved. In the case of GE Capital's acquisition of Gelco (at that time, it was GE Capital's largest acquisition), a senior human-resources executive who had been involved in the due diligence effort was asked to stay on and support the newly acquired Gelco team. He acted as a facilitator to the new leadership team; brought groups of people from GE Capital and Gelco together in work sessions to develop common plans; oriented the new team to GE Capital's requirements; made sure that the soft sides of the integration (such as communication and benefits) were taken into account; and counselled Gelco's senior managers about how to succeed in GE Capital.[lxv]

The Gelco integration had gone well. However, GE Capital had not yet recognized the role of the integration manager until several other acquisitions that had no integration managers failed to proceed as smoothly. In one instance, after a unit had failed to meet expectations, a re-integration effort which included a fulltime integration manager was undertaken and the situation was turned around. By 1994, the role of an integration manager became intentional strategy. [lxvi]

In their experience, the most effective integration managers were those that had served on the due diligence team and who aside from possessing technical skills, also possessed personal characteristics such as strong inter-personal skills and sensitivity to cultural differences, ability to facilitate groups, deep knowledge of how GE Capital works and energy to do what it takes to make integration successful. Their integration managers were held accountable for the creation and delivery of a disciplined integration plan and for reaching the plan's milestones. [lxvii]

The identification of skilled integration leaders is important to help the companies not only integrate but also to help the combined companies conduct their business as usual. As observed by Kummer, during integration, it is difficult not to be overly occupied with oneself, but to serve the customers as well. There might be even some extra worries to overcome in the usual operations as well. For example, former customers might rather turn to and buy from competitors, because customers would know what to expect from the competitors while the merging company is in unrest. [lxviii]

Kummer also states that from a management capability point of view, companies need to have enough in-house people who are experienced with the merger and acquisition situation and process in order to do a meaningful PMI. [lxix]

Chevriere, on the other hand states that the highest level of the integration team spells out the ground rules governing the effort of constructing a new company. This means spelling out in clear language the financial and operational assumptions the integration team will use and setting out the objectives of the integration process, the schedule, and the organizational design criteria. [lxx]

A top management team has to be set up to provide strategic direction and develop these ground rules. This team usually includes the chief executives of the two firms and their most trusted deputies. They, in turn, have to nominate the right person for the post of "integration chief executive." There is also a need to nominate key personnel for the business process and business support team that will porform the hard nuts-and-bolts work of combining the two firms. [lxxi]

SPEED

Again, from the GE Capital experience, Ashkenas and his colleagues state that decisions about management structure, key roles, reporting relationships, layoffs, restructuring, and other career affecting aspects of the integration should be made, announced and implemented as soon as possible after the deal is signed – within days, if possible. The reason for this is that creeping changes, uncertainty and anxiety that last for months are debilitating and immediately start to drain value from an acquisition. [lxxii]

It was observed that acquiring managers close the deal with a certain amount of euphoria, ready to get on with the exciting challenge of running the new business better, but staff members from the acquired company who are needed to keep things running and make improvements are preoccupied with issues of security and identity. They have no interest in a close-the-deal party; they just want to know if they still have jobs. If left unrecognized, this psychodrama can be debilitating and can send the integration process down the wrong path. [lxxiii]

Moreover, when issues of security are not addressed immediately, levels of productivity, customer service, and innovation quickly deteriorate as employees focus on their own needs rather than on those of the company. If acquiring managers restructure quickly but without sensitivity, they risk beginning their tenure without the trust and respect of the remaining staff. The challenge is to avoid both traps, to make structural changes as quickly as possible but in a way that maintains everyone's dignity. If that challenge is not met, successful integration may not be possible. [lxxiv]

Also, there were times when GE capital had to reduce staff or lay off workers as cost reduction measures. Yet, these important moves would be delayed probably due to fear that they would be seen as the "bad guys." However, when they did get around to the difficult part of laying off people, it turned out that the staff from the acquired company usually asked – "Why only now?"

The message gleaned from that reaction is that "change is inevitable, let's get on with it rather than allow anxiety and speculation to diffuse energy and focus." [lxxv]

Kummer states that the identification of key people that should be retained also can take place early on. This process should be guided again by the strategy: Why has this deal been done in the first place? What are its strategic and operational aims? These answers will help to answer the questions: Who are the people that have a significant impact on the future value of the company? Who are the people that possess critical capabilities, competencies and relationships for the future success of the business? [lxxvi]

That, speed is essential in PMI was confirmed by a PricewaterhouseCoopers study. In their 2009 study dealing with European corporations that had been involved in mergers and acquisitions, more than 60% of respondents thought that the integration took too long. Reasons for wanting a faster integration are the potential cost savings, realising synergies sooner and the reduction of employee uncertainty. However, there were also respondents who preferred a slower integration mainly due to the complexity of the IT integration as well as by delaying non-critical integration processes. [lxxvii]

TRANSPARENCY AND RESPECT IN THE RESTRUCTURING PROCESS

Drawing from the experiences of GE Capital, Ashkenas, et al. state that the acquiring company should be straightforward about what is happening and what is planned. Even when the news is bad, staff of newly acquired companies appreciate the truth. That includes being able to say "we don't know" about certain areas or "we have not yet decided" about others. It also includes sharing information about when and by what process a decision may be reached. [lxxviii]

It means acknowledging stress and emotions involved in the restructuring process, not telling them that all will be business as usual when they are confused, and that it was a merger of equals when they had been taken over. It includes treating those individuals who will be negatively affected with dignity, respect, and support. Not only is it the correct thing to do, it shows to those who remain, about what kind of company they now are working for. This, in turn, helps them to develop positive feelings. [lxxix]

PEOPLE STRATEGY AND MELDING OF CULTURES

As stated earlier in this work, a lot of merger failures are attributed to the failure to harmonize differences in corporate culture. A commonly cited example is that of Daimler Chrysler where differences in corporate culture were either ignored or not addressed. This contributed to the failure of the merged entity to achieve expected synergies and eventually led to a break up of the once celebrated merger.

What can be done to integrate cultures? And are culture differences truly obstacles to merger success?

CORPORATE CULTURE DEFINED

Culture has been defined as the pattern of norms, values, beliefs, and attitudes that influence individual and group behavior within an organization. Originating with the founders of the organization, these norms, values, and beliefs are shaped and honed over time by senior executives and other stakeholders. These values filter down through the organization, further refined and modified in the day-to-day priorities and actions of all the managers and employees in the business. They then, circle back up the organization, reinforcing and refining the thinking of senior managers. Culture is "the way we do things" and includes factors such as:
- How we treat our customers, suppliers, and each other
- The type and level of participation in decision-making
- The level, speed, and process of decision-making
- The level of formality and controls
- Performance rewards
- Risk tolerance
- Quality and cost orientation [lxxx]

The term 'corporate culture' is used to describe issues like objectives, personal interests, behavior, etc. Many problems in co-operation and teamwork are blamed on culture. In a merger, 'culture' is more than making the people from both partners work together smoothly. The development of a new, shared culture is a critical factor for merger success. [lxxxi]

Corporate culture is not an independent variable in the business equation. Rather, culture exists, or should exist, to support the business strategy. Culture is the power that binds people together. Organizationally, it provides a common thread for day-to-day activities and offers consistency in a turbulent environment. [lxxxii]

Recklies states that there is no one right culture for an organization, but there are only cultures that fit more or less to the particular situation of the organization. Also, several cultures can exist within one organization. He points out that there are three types of cultural differences:
- Cross-national differences (especially in cross-border mergers),
- Cross-organizational differences
- Cross-functional differences. [lxxxiii]

He explains that in practice, problems of cultural fit can be found in the following areas:
- Organizational values
- Management culture and leadership styles
- Organizational myths and stories
- Organizational taboos, rituals
- Cultural symbols

He states further that cultural problems can develop unexpected dynamics in such situations:
1. Realization of differences
2. Stressing and evaluation of differences
3. Mutual stereotyping
4. Mutual blaming
5. Battle for cultural dominance [lxxxiv]

IMPORTANCE OF CORPORATE CULTURE

The importance of corporate culture cannot be overlooked. The correlation between productivity and a culture that had been managed is clear. A Harvard Business School study showing that firms that "actively managed" their corporate cultures realized a 682 percent increase in revenue compared with a 166 percent increase for firms that did not manage culture. Net income increased 757 percent for the firms that attended to culture versus a 1 percent increase for those that did not. Also, stock prices soared 901 percent for firms that actively managed their cultures, while those that did not realized only a 74 percent rise in stock price. [lxxxv]

Corporate culture influences the performance of an organization, since it determines:
- The way the organization tackles problems and questions
- Peoples' attitude to changes
- The way people interact with each other
- The way the organization interacts with stakeholders
- Peoples' commitment to strategy[lxxxvi]

MELDING CULTURES

In mergers, an AT Kearney study shows that a problem in many mergers is that the more powerful partner imposes his culture on the less powerful one. This is done without any evaluation which culture would be the more suitable one for the new organization. This approach may lead to a successful merger and integration quickly in some situations. In other situations, however, this approach destroys much of the value that was expected to grow from the merger especially when both partners are very different. Such a situation needs a closer evaluation as to which culture would be best for both together. [lxxxvii]

Ashkenas and his colleagues state that an important lesson that they learned from GE Capital acquisitions is that successful integration melds not only the various technical aspects of the businesses but also the different cultures. The best way to do so is to get people working together quickly to solve business problems and accomplish results that could not have been achieved before. [lxxxviii]

Ashkenas likens an acquisition to an arranged marriage where the "parents" negotiate the deal, sign the contract, and then expect the "newlyweds" to live together in harmony. However, an arranged marriage has a much better chance of success than an acquisition does since only one couple is involved, and the parties usually come from similar cultures and share common values. The same does not hold true in acquisitions, where many people – sometimes thousands – need to learn how to live together and the values and mindsets of the acquiring and acquired organizations almost always differ. That disparity is even more marked when the two companies are based in different national cultures. [lxxxix]

Recklies states that cultural pluralism and cultural blending do not work in most cases. The results are cultural resistance followed by a cultural takeover (the AT Kearney finding). [xc]

Ashkenas recounts that GE Capital distilled four steps which business leaders can take to bridge the cultural gaps that exist when integrating any acquisition.
- Meet, greet, and plan (urgently).
- Communicate, communicate –and then communicate some more.
- Address the cultural issues head on.
- Move from the few to the many, cascade the integration process.[xci]

Oliver Recklies, on the other hand, suggests the following steps for cultural integration:
- Develop a strategy for cultural integration already in pre-merger phase. Decide if you want to go on with one of the existing cultures or if you prefer an integration culture.
- Analyze and describe the existing cultures. Differences and common elements of both cultures show up only in direct comparison. Thus, you can also identify cultural barriers, differences in communication and other potential problems.
- Decide which role the new culture shall play in the merged organization. Determine, why you decide for a particular culture and what you want to achieve with it.
- Establish 'bridges' between both companies. In order to achieve mutual understanding, there is nothing better than co-operation.
- Establish a basis and mechanisms for the new culture. This includes a supporting system of rewards and sanctions.
- Be patient. People take time to get acquainted to a new cultural reality. [xcii]

Other studies on the other hand, have identified various stages of culture integration for international M&A as contact, conflict, adaptation and integration. [xciii]

At the contact stage, teams in both acquired and acquiring companies explore each other's product, management style, corporate culture as well as reputation of the company. They identify the common grounds and the gaps in perception of version, value, structure, management practices and behaviour, strengths and weaknesses of both companies in human resource and areas that may cause conflicts between the staff. The culture gap analysis may be done through questionnaires, discussions, interviews, focus groups, etc. Information obtained at this stage may be used to devise an integration plan suited to the companies. [xciv]

The second stage is the stage of conflict. It is at this point where the integration plan is implemented. Different values may cause problems such as social comparison, stereotyping. From the national culture level, differences can arise from language and underlying cultural value. On the other hand, differences arising from corporate culture may occur from differences in management style and core values. Culture conflicts could go through a three-stage process - - magnifying differences, stereotyping differences and putting down. If this happens, the result will be disappointment, anger and stress from the team that had been put down. Those working in a foreign country would be surrounded by a different language and culture and may face loneliness and emotional stress. They start to be evocative of the culture in their country and thus unable to integrate into the culture of the organization. [xcv]

To avoid such conflict, analysts suggest that organizations conduct cultural awareness training for its staff to increase staff's communications from both acquiring and acquired companies, to understand each other's culture from a bias-free perspective. Activities such as team work, role playing and practical training may be undertaken to break through individual's stereotype of the other culture and to find out the differences more effectively and therefore more easily to adopt into each other's culture. [xcvi]

It is also important to resolve conflicts immediately after they explode by understanding the problem through formal and informal discussion, following up the result after implementation of the resolution, and adjusting the implication appropriately accordingly. [xcvii]

The third stage of culture integration is the adopting stage. As cultures on both national and corporate levels are embedded in history and values that are psychologically rooted in people, there may be strong resistance for any changes. At this stage both teams should actively be involved in understanding and adapting to each other's culture. Through active communication and adjustment, they will allow the organization to form a range of new management style and structure that suits both cultures. [xcviii]

The last stage is the integration stage. In international M&A situations, the organization needs to take into account its environment when developing a new corporate culture. For example, it needs to rethink its social and market environment, operational strategy and direction, as well as the strength from both acquiring and acquired companies, in order to develop a culture that could enable the organization to take advantage of its strength and thus to be competitive. National and corporate culture differences may lead to failure. However, it can also be a competitive advantage. If management can actively be involved in learning the culture of others, it will increase organization's ability to adapt to its environment, look at problem-solving and decision-making from different perspectives and become more flexible in its management style for its employees worldwide. [xcix]

Steven H. Appelbaum, Jesse Roberts and Barbara T. Shapiro discuss and contrast the cultural fit, cultural potential, communication, direction, and leadership in the success and failures of mergers and acquisitions. They state that many acquirers need to understand that in an acquisition, it is not the assets, technology, or infrastructure that is difficult to assess and integrate before, during, and after the takeover, but it is more the people. Failure to fully assess the compatibility of cultures in the outset, the potential for compatibility in the future, is unknowingly decreasing their success from the outset. They assert that the cultural fit, cultural potential, communication, and direction in the pre/during/post stages of an acquisition are very important.[c]

Appelbaum, Roberts and Shapiro explain that the cultural fit seeks similarities in style, leadership, direction, communication, and organization policies. It is not imperative that a company must have similar cultures, but it is definitely a hurdle if they are so very different from one another, requiring extra time, attention, and communication in order to integrate the two. [ci]

They cite management stylistics as another critical issue in the cultural fit between the two firms. If the preferences for style of management, degrees and ways of planning, formalization, rewards and sanction modes, time perspectives and growth orientations point in the same direction, it is easier to design an integrative structure than when preferences are far apart. [cii]

Cultural potential is the framework in which companies operate, including cultural traits that guide the way in which relations with other organizations and cultures are handled. [ciii]

It is an excellent barometer and reveals openness to change, mainly affecting the following traits:

1. Innovative Potential: openness to new values and ideas;
2. Trust Potential: openness to trust;
3. Mutual Dependence Potential: the mindset of two companies working together for the greater good; and
4. Integrative Potential: the openness of a company to sorting through issues, understanding differences, and wanting to work through differences. [civ]

With respect to the aspect of communication, direction, and leadership, Appelbaum and his colleagues say that it is difficult to separate communication, direction, and leadership, since they are concentric. Each has their part to play in the stages of an acquisition, and neither can happen without the other. The direction and leadership of a company is one thing, but in the midst of an acquisition, a new style of leadership and direction is needed and time and effort are further required to create open avenues of communication and information. [cv]

With respect to leadership, tactics should include establishing leadership immediately for a smoother integration process. As for direction and communication, they suggest that the top management help employees cope with the loss they are experiencing to decrease the chance of M&A failure and cultural clash and to increase employees overall adjustment. They state that employees exhibit strong negative emotions upon the announcement of a merger in terms synonymous with the death of a family member or loved one. They cite the example of Cisco Systems which establishes a buddy system - someone to go to during the early days of integration—to help the employee feel at ease and a part of Cisco Systems. [cvi]

Delays in communication only create increased anxiety, stress, negatively affecting future relations and trust. Silence is interpreted negatively as a sign of weak leadership and unclear goals. Employees are looking for answers to the "me" type of questions—How does the merger affect me? What will be my role in the new organization? Why should I sign up to the new vision and strategy? [cvii]

They state that M&A's should not be considered as only a legal and/or financial transaction but rather a process in which the lives of people are affected.

Even employees who are fully willing to invest their energy in making the new structure work often find themselves at a loss about the "hows" in situations of unclear expectations. Clear goals and expectations are necessary for the current and future direction of the organization as a whole. [cviii]

They emphasize that a vision must be clearly communicated to the new organization with very clear lines on how and where the new company is going. Creating the change is necessary, as companies that can change have an inherent competitive advantage over their competition [cix]

CULTURAL ISSUES MAY BE OVERSTATED

One analyst asserts that although there are a lot of cultural challenges which might affect the final outcome of a PMI; he is personally convinced that these issues are sometimes completely overstated. He states that culture is a good scapegoat and relatively easy to blame, because qualitative and soft issues are hard to disprove. This line of argumentation helps to distract attention from other major mistakes that have been made earlier in the M&A process, such as in strategy making. [cx]

He states that challenges in the cultural dimension can result from the several different spheres of culture all at once. The first dimension of culture is geographical culture. This is the most obvious case of culture issues in deals, i.e., cross-border deals, where the acquirer or merging partners might experience differences due to different national cultures. However, even in domestic deals, there may be a clash of cultures originating from regional differences in culture. [cxi]

The next dimension is corporate culture. Differences in corporate culture might make integration very slow and costly and could create an inefficient new organization. As an example, Kummer gives the combination of two companies from two different industries with different industrial cultures such as banking and insurance or the diversification or forward integration toward distributors or clients. He notes that differences in industrial cultures can exist within the same industry. For instance, investment banking and private banking are totally different segments that are very likely to follow completely different philosophies. [cxii]

The last dimension relates to functional/professional cultures. For example, IT people will get along more easily with other IT people than from finance people. In a PMI situation, this would create additional obstacles as the companies will have to tackle integration across all functions. [cxiii]

Kummer says that the actual cultural integration approach is interlinked to the chosen PMI approach:

- *Cultural preservation* keeps the entities apart and maintains their cultures.
- *Acculturation* adapts the culture from one of the companies.
- *Best of both worlds* blends the best of cultures.
- *New culture* tries to create a completely new corporate culture. [cxiv]

Kummer observes that, as these challenges in cultures are most likely to exist in every transaction, cultural effects should be priced into the valuation of the combined entity and any expected synergies (or rather dis-synergies). Pricing these cultural issues into valuation certainly is very difficult, but possible to do. This can be done for example in the following ways to quantify them in terms of:

- The risk for the return on a transaction (a higher expectation on risk premium in valuation)
- The effect on operational productivity in the business plan (probably a drop)
- A budget to explore the cultural differences (investment during due diligence [cxv])

EFFECTIVE PMI

Based on the preceding discussions, we can glean the following principles:

1. PMI should start even before the merger process is instituted or at the due diligence stage;
2. PMIs need to be tailored to suit the needs of each combination;
3. PMI processes should have effective leaders and managers;

4. PMI is not just a matter of harmonizing procedures, physical equipment, financials and legal matters. It is a matter of bringing people from differing cultures to work together in harmony. Melding cultures is important if a merger is to be a success.
5. PMI works best when done in a transparent and open environment – meaning communication is done effectively and honestly as truth is valued;
6. Speed in implementation of PMI is vital in ensuring merger success.

Where there is effective PMI, there would be more obvious synergies achieved. Shareholder value would be enhanced and the M&A could be deemed a success.

PART III – THE AUTHOR'S OWN STORY

You may ask, how have I seen the principles of effective PMI at work in my own business life?

I have been through a number of mergers and acquisitions – either on the side of the acquiring company or the acquired business. I have also taken part in M&A's on the part of the management side and seen it from the point of view of an employee.

I have seen the effects of lack of transparency and effective communication and how it can negatively affect employees of an acquired corporation. In one corporation where I worked as a manager, a major shareholder who was also in management assured us that it would be "business as usual" even after our corporation had been acquired. We took him by his word and thus were surprised when the new shareholder and management suddenly put in their own team members to operate the corporation.

The former management had lied to us and we lost our faith in the corporation because of the lack of truthful information. We felt that we could not trust the new management.

It proved to be disastrous. The new management was not able to regain our trust. Shortly after the introduction of the new team members, I left and so did most of my staff. We carried with us a lot of knowledge and information and invaluable talent and experience. In the meantime, it turned out that the new shareholder was not familiar with the corporation's business, nearly running it to the ground and decimating shareholder value in the process.

The communication should have been honest, transparent and frank. I found that people need certainty and clarity during this period. Good people or those that you want to retain will be the first to exit if the communication channels are not clear. They may have the misunderstanding that they will be the next ones on the chopping block. Even rats will desert a sinking ship.

In this case, the new shareholder could have prevented the exodus and utilized the combined talents and experience of the staff to enhance the business operations if he had taken the simple step of truthfully informing the staff about changes in the organization even before he brought in his new management team.

In another case, it was a matter of cultural misfit. I was working for a listed group that was highly bureaucratic and formal in its business dealings. It acquired a family run business which was making good money. We required the owner and founder of the family - run business, to submit management reports, attend meetings and abide by proper approval limits and comply with standard operating procedures.

The owner and founder were naturally upset, having run the business in a more informal and independent way which had worked in the past. He wanted mainly to be left alone. There was tension which would erupt in petty quarrels or create misunderstandings. Of course, the business suffered and in the end, the listed company divested and the business reverted to the owner just to cut losses for both sides.

Perhaps, if my employer had exercised a little more diligence in examining what would be the best way to integrate the business into its own operations, it could have saved the transaction. Or better still, it could have first conducted a cultural due diligence that could have revealed the cultural misfit. My employer could have walked away from the deal and saved valuable time, money and goodwill. Or, it could have chosen the path of being a mere investor without taking active part in the management or operations.

Not all the mergers that I have participated in have ended unhappily. I once worked for a corporation engaged in the oil industry. In this particular case, our corporation had been dealing with an upstream supplier for many years. The 'marriage' was kind of a natural next step since both had been considering a merger for many years. It was a vertical merger where we bought into our upstream supplier. Because of the familiarity born out of many years of dealing with each other, integration was not difficult.

On another occasion, while I was employed with a GE US affiliate that merged with another manufacturer, I was privileged to see the famous GE Capital acquisition methodology put to work. Both parties in the transaction were able to secure mutual trust by being transparent right from the very start about what they could do and what they could not do. The most important thing was that staff of the acquired corporation was immediately informed whether they were going to be retained or displaced. In this case, I found out that it was true that people are not against bad news, but they want to see quick results and prefer closure rather than uncertainty.

In other instances, I was involved in mergers where independent integration consultants were brought in to facilitate the integration. These specialists were objective and not bogged down by past packages or prejudices. The acquired company also felt more comfortable dealing with these integration consultants as they were objective and focused on the integration process. Because of the objectivity of the specialists, potential clashes arising from cultural differences or competition or resistance to change were minimized or even avoided.

What I can say is that if companies create a plan to handle integration issues even before the merger takes place, in addition to studying the financial and strategic fits, mergers would be more successful. When the merger kicks in, all parties are clear on what to do. And where there is clarity, it is easier to operate a business and maintain or even enhance shareholder value.

PART IV

SOME MERGER INTEGRATION STORIES

This part of the e-book focuses on the M & A experiences of global giants.

FIRST STORY: THE GE CAPITAL CULTURAL INTEGRATION EXPERIENCE [cxvi]

As stated earlier in this e-book, GE Capital distilled four steps in effective cultural integration:
- Meet, greet, and plan (urgently).
- Communicate, communicate –and then communicate some more.
- Address the cultural issues head on.
- Move from the few to the many, cascade the integration process.[cxvii]

STEP ONE: MEET, GREET, AND PLAN (URGENTLY) FOR THE FIRST 100 DAYS

Once a deal is closed and transfer of ownership becomes official, the GE Capital business leader, with the help of the acquisition manager, organizes orientation and planning sessions for members of the management teams of the new acquisition and in GE Capital to fulfil the following purposes:

- Create a 100-day plan for acquisition integration.
- Welcome new senior managers into GE Capital and give them a chance to socialize with their new colleagues.
- Provide an opportunity for both sides to exchange information and share their feelings and reactions about the recently completed deal. [cxviii]

In the orientation and planning sessions, newly acquired managers talk about their organization, products, people, and plans and in particular the positive aspects of their company – what they feel good about and what should be built upon. They also share their thoughts about opportunities for improvement – what could be changed, areas of potential growth, and synergies with GE Capital. [cxix]

In response, the GE Capital business leader, the integration manager, and other executives describe what it means to be a part of GE Capital – the values, the responsibilities, the challenges, and the rewards. They also present and discuss standards required of a GE Capital business unit, including a list of approximately 25 policies and practices that need to be incorporated into the way the acquired company does business. [cxx]

Based on the standards set by GE Capital and the opportunities for improvement presented by the acquired management team, they draft a 100- day plan for acquisition and integration which addresses issues such as the need for integrating functions, taking steps necessary for financial and procedural compliance, making shifts in compensation and benefits, and managing customer contacts. [cxxi]

The 100-day timetable creates a sense of urgency, challenge, and excitement and imbues the integration with a feeling of zest and energy. It also forces the management team to move into action and avoid becoming paralyzed by mixed feelings and personal politics. [cxxii]

STEP TWO: COMMUNICATE, COMMUNICATE – AND THEN COMMUNICATE SOME MORE.

During the due diligence and negotiation phases, GE Capital creates a communication plan so that employees and external parties are informed as soon as a deal is closed. After that, they

create forums for dialogue and interaction between the acquirer and acquiree. The four considerations in their communications plan are:
- Audience
- Timing
- Mode and
- Message. [cxxiii]

They cite their integration effort with GE Capital's Private Label Credit Card business as an example on how a communication plan was executed:

- AUDIENCE: Several distinct audiences were identified: the senior managers of both organizations; the integration manager and his team; all of the employees of the acquired organization; all of GE Capital's employees; the customers, clients, and vendors of the combined company; the community; and the media.

- TIMING: The appropriate time to communicate with each audience was identified: for instance if it should be before the deal was closed,, at closing, or perhaps 60 days after the closing.

- MODE OF COMMUNICATION: Depending upon the type of audience, they selected the appropriate mode of communication, ranging from newsletters and memos to videos to small-group huddles to town meetings and visits from management.

The fundamental message they wished to convey was that, at GE Capital:
- Communication and involvement are valued and considered to be critical success factors;
- GE Capital does not hide information from employees;
- GE Capital wants to create a relationship of trust and open dialogue across all boundaries in the organization. [cxxiv]

Ashkenas said that managers and not professional communicators, took the lead in many aspects of the process to engage in dialogue with their employees, peers, customers, and others. The 100-day plan itself was disseminated so that everyone was given an opportunity to learn about its broad outlines. GE Capital assumed that   the more people knew about what was happening, the more they would be able to accept change and overcome their cultural and historical differences. [cxxv]

STEP THREE: ADDRESS THE CULTURAL ISSUES HEAD ON

As GE Capital made more acquisitions outside the United States, it realized that a number of unrecognized cultural issues which rooted indifferences in corporate culture were magnified and complicated by differences in national culture.

For instance, in countries with hierarchical social systems, the issue of deference to authority prevented managers from challenging, questioning, and thus enriching GE Capital's ideas about how to grow the new business.

In some settings, seemingly straightforward instructions were misinterpreted not only because of language barriers but also because of assumptions about intentions. In still other cases, GE

Capital found that newly acquired leaders did not comfortably accept the autonomy that comes along with empowerment. [cxxvi]

Ashkenas relates that together with a consulting firm, GE capital constructed a systematic process of cross-cultural analysis leading up to a structured three-day "cultural workout" session between GE Capital and the newly acquired management team. Using results of focus groups and interviews with customers and employees, a computer-generated analysis was developed that plotted the acquired company's culture on a scattergram across four dimensions: costs, technology, brands, and customers. And contrasts how employees see the company with the way customers see it. A similar survey was done for the GE Capital business. [cxxvii]

Once, survey results were out, managers from both GE Capital and the acquired company met for a three-day cultural workout. Results were compared to highlight areas of convergence and differences. Participants, with a facilitator, then went through the data, shared their thoughts on why the results turned out the way they did, the history of their companies, the folklore and the heroes that made them what they are. That would lead to focused discussions about cultural differences and similarities and their implications for doing business like how to go to market, how much to focus on cost, or how concepts of authority differ. [cxxviii]

By the third day of the session, participants shifted their focus from the past to the future. Based on what had been accomplished in the first 100 days, they were asked two questions:
- Where do they want to take the company?
- What kind of future do they want to create?

That discussion resulted in a written outline of a new business plan for the acquired company based on the goals that were established as part of the original deal augmented by the collective dreams and aspirations of the new management team. [cxxix]

STEP FOUR: MOVE FROM THE FEW TO THE MANY, CASCADE THE INTEGRATION PROCESS.

To bridge cultures beyond the management team, GE Capital developed the following approaches:
- Share results of the cultural workout and discuss the results through small group meetings, videos, and other channels.
- Assign short term projects that focus on achieving results quickly and include staff members from both GE Capital and the acquired company. The faster people from both companies are given opportunities to work together on important business issues, the faster integration will occur. [cxxx]

The second strategy was used with great effect in 1995, when GE Capital's Global Consumer Finance business acquired Minebea Financial, a Japanese financial-services company. A number of joint GCF Minebea teams were commissioned to accomplish critical business goals in the first 100 days.

One team reduced the cost of materials through an initiative aimed at having the suppliers manage inventory. Another arranged for the sale of written-off receivables. Still another reduced the time it took to respond to customers' telephone calls from three minutes to ten seconds. [cxxxi]

Equally as important as the results were what the people from GCF and Minebea learned by working together was that by achieving results quickly, they immediately saw the benefits of the acquisition – that more could be achieved together than could ever have been accomplished separately. [cxxxii]

EXPERIMENTS ON AN INDIVIDUAL LEVEL

On the individual level, GE Capital experiments in other ways to help their people deal with differences in national cultures. For instance, an American assigned to lead a key function in India could be individually coached by an external consultant who specializes in national cultures. High potential leaders are included in a program called the Capital University where middle managers are given 6-12 month assignments in a GE Capital business or head-office function in the United States. Middle managers with their families are also coached individually by consultants about differences in national cultures. [cxxxiii]

The GE Capital experience has been so successful that it has been studied by experts and copied by other integration experts. It is believed that with a few adjustments, GE Capital had found an integration methodology that could work with most corporations even across borders.

SECOND STORY: DAIMLERCHRYSLER – FAILED CULTURAL INTEGRATION

This story, on the other hand, illustrates the disastrous effects of a cultural misalignment.

In 1998, Daimler-Benz purchased Chrysler, a highly profitable U.S. automaker enjoying record sales of light trucks, vans and large sedans. Three years later, Chrysler was hemorrhaging money, market capitalization of the combined DaimlerChrysler had not budged and expected synergies with its new German parent company were nowhere to be found. According to numerous observers, what happened amounted to a textbook case of cultural misalignment. [cxxxiv]

Chrysler saw itself as a bold innovator of vehicles for middle-class Americans and a plucky survivor of four brushes with near-bankruptcy. Daimler, on the other hand, stood for uncompromising quality and disciplined German engineering. The two companies distrusted one another from the start, to the point that some Daimler executives publicly vowed that they would never be seen in a Chrysler vehicle. Distrust likely fuelled the business woes that faced the partnership, such as the fierce resistance by Daimler executives to link product development across the two organizations. [cxxxv]

One analyst observed that the merged organization operated like two independent companies that simply added together their numbers on the balance sheet—and not much else. The cultural divide was reflected not only in the two groups' products but also in their management styles. Daimler-Benz fostered a formal, highly structured work environment; Chrysler took pride in its more relaxed, free-wheeling approach. [cxxxvi]

Not surprisingly, as Daimler asserted dominance over the combined companies, Chrysler began a steep downturn, with widespread departures among key executives and engineers, growing discontent among the rank-and-file, and mounting hostility between Stuttgart and Detroit. [cxxxvii]

After nearly a decade of organizational turmoil and plunging profits, Daimler sold its Chrysler division in May 2007, formally dissolving a union hailed as one of the worst mergers in history. [cxxxviii]

Even during the negotiations, cultural issues were already present such as the leading role to be played by Daimler Benz versus the notion of a merger of equals; location of the corporate domicile (in Germany); and corporate name (Daimler's name came before Chrysler). Analysts state that the ramifications of the way these issues were "negotiated" prevented the new entity from functioning as an integrated unit. [cxxxix]

During the transition, the following culture fit issues arose:

1. *Executive compensations*: Americans were used to larger salaries;
2. *Business Travel*: Daimler-Benz employees flew first-class in keeping with the company's luxury image while only top officers of Chrysler could fly first-class. What seemed a mundane issue became a major source of conflict that took over six months to resolve.
3. *Work habits and styles:* Daimler embraced formality and hierarchy, from its intricately structured decision-making processes to its suit-and-tie dress code and respect for titles and proper names; Chrysler disregarded barriers and promoted cross-functional teams that favored open collars, free-form discussions, and casual repartee. Daimler executives had larger staffs and fatter expense accounts; Chrysler officers had broader responsibilities and bigger salaries and bonuses. Germans smoked, drank wine with lunch, and worked late hours. Chrysler banned smoking and alcohol in its facilities. The Americans worked around the clock on deadlines but did not stay late as a routine.
4. *Decision making process*: At Daimler, the German employees' decisions worked their way to the top of the hierarchy through formal channels and then they were set in stone. At Chrysler, the executives allowed mid-level managers to proceed on their own initiatives, sometimes without waiting for executive level approval
5. *Financial reporting system*: German accounting system is vastly different--companies and stockholders focus on full-year results—companies crank up the numbers in the fourth quarter to make the strong numbers; U.S. Financial reporting system is on a quarterly basis, and is sleekly efficient . [cxl]

Commentators stated that they didn't just make cars differently, they lived in different worlds— cultural differences extended beyond attitudes and styles. [cxli]

One year into the new operation, the Chairman of the merged company, Jűrgen Schrempp fired Thomas Stallkamp, president of the company's U.S. arm who was also responsible for the integration of the two companies and reduced the management board from 17 to 13 with the result that there were eight Germans and five Americans on the board. He further created three vehicle divisions; Chrysler Brands headed by James Holden (Stallkamp's replacement), Mercedes-Benz Division, and the Commercial Truck Division. Only a third of the top executives of Chrysler remained with the merged company and, Robert Eaton, co-chairman of DaimlerChrysler made it clear that he would retire within three years. [cxlii]

In October 2000, in an interview reported in the Financial Times, Jűrgen Schrempp seemed to boast of deceiving the Chrysler management into thinking that the merger was to be of equals and the two companies would be integrated prompting major investor, Kirk Kerkorian, to file a lawsuit against DaimlerChrysler. Following this controversy, Schrempp fired James Holden, the last president of DaimlerChrysler ostensibly for huge financial losses in the U.S. operations. Schrempp was later reported to have stated Holden's dismissal was more due to cultural differences rather than financial performance. Designers also left the organization. With the dismissal of James Holden and the appointment of Dieter Zetsche as his replacement, practically all the top Chrysler leaders had quit, or had been fired and it seemed that the major reason for the merger had been lost - Chrysler's management expertise in mass car building to overcome Daimler's weakness in its capability to meet the needs of the emerging auto markets. [cxliii]

In fact, by 2000, DaimlerChrysler leadership, delayed or shelved several of Chrysler Division's most promising products including the 300 sedan project. One of Chrysler's competitive advantages, being quick to market with interesting designs, also seemed to be lost. [cxliv]

To counter the above situations, jobs were eliminated, Jeep and large car product development teams were combined with the objective of working closely on under skin components to save money. In 2004, Chrysler Division started to show signs of a sustained comeback. Chrysler Division freely admitted the contribution of its German partner with shared operating and production systems, communization of air bags, heating, ventilation and air conditioning systems. However, the feeling was not mutual. By 2007, Daimler sold its interest in Chrysler to an equity group. [cxlv]

Appelbaum, Roberts and Shapiro analyzed the Daimler-Chrysler merger as follows: [cxlvi]

Case #1: Daimler-Chrysler (Failure)

Cultural Fit:	Not a good one. Chrysler had a reputation for having a more freewheeling, open culture, in contrast with the more traditional, top-down management style practiced by Daimler. Daimler-Benz was synonymous with words like conservative, efficient and safe. Chrysler, in contrast was known as daring, diverse and creative.
Cultural Potential: Innovative	Yes, the Germans admired the entrepreneurial spirit and innovative thinking of the Chrysler team while Chrysler respected the engineering savvy of the Germans.
Cultural Potential: Trust	Not much. Several of the key executives who had led Chrysler to a solid reputation for creativity, efficiency and profitability retired early or defected to other car makers feeling uncertainty and no trust/confidence in the new corporation.
Cultural Potential: Mutual Dependence	No, this was negatively affected when Juegen Schrempp, the ex-chairman of Daimler-Benz moved members of his German management team into key Chrysler positions signalling the lack of intent to share the vision. The management teams resisted to work together and were not willing to compromise so that Daimler and Chrysler had combined not much beyond some administrative departments, such as finance and public relations. Components and platforms were also not shared early enough because Mercedes-Benz executives worried that their buyers might feel cheated if they shared parts with Chrysler's "inferior technology".

Cultural Potential: Integrative	No information could be quantifiable.
Communication	(Since the merger, DaimlerChrysler chairman Juergen Schrempp has acknowledged in a newspaper review that the so-called merger of equals was, in fact, a capture of Chrysler by Daimler-Benz.
Direction	No information could be quantifiable
Leadership	No information could be quantifiable.

Despite the perceived potentials and the synergies of two auto giants, the Daimler –Chrysler merger failed. From the story, it appears that the German counterpart wished to impose its culture on its American counterpart which of course could not be done seeing that the American corporation had a proud history of its own not to mention that it came from a country that has a strong national identity and sense of self. It could probably have worked had there been more willingness on the part of Daimler to give up some of its "Germnanness" and embrace a part of the American culture that had made Chrysler a successful automaker prior to the merger.

THIRD STORY: LENOVO -- A SUCCESS STORY IN THE MAKING?

As of the writing of this e-book, it seems that many eyes are on the founder of Lenovo which is conducting a grand experiment called the "Lenovo Way."

Lenovo started out as the Legend in a one–story shop in Beijing which grew to be a global manufacturer of personal computers with principal offices located in the US, China, Singapore as well as research centers in the US, Japan and China.

It was formed in 1984 by Liu Chuanzhi along with ten computer scientists. They envisioned a company that would bring the advantages of information technology to the Chinese people. [cxlvii]

Using seed money from the China Academy of Sciences (Mr. Liu had worked with CAS and had been able to convince them to open another computer corporation), Legend imported a wide range of equipment which included roller skates, color televisions and electronic watches although the latter items were early flops. [cxlviii]

It also introduced PCs to households and promoted PC usage in China by establishing retail shops nationwide. In 1985, it developed the pioneering Legend Chinese Character Card that translated English operating software into Chinese characters. Later, it achieved breakthroughs like PCs with one-button access to the Internet. [cxlix]

In 1990, it launched its very first Legend PC in the market. Legend changed its role from that of an agent for imported computer products into that of a producer and seller of its own branded computer products. [cl]

In 1994, Legend was listed and traded on the Hong Kong Stock Exchange. By 1996, it became the market share leader in China for the first time. In 1998, it produced its one-millionth personal computer. [cli]

In 2003, Legend changed its brand name to Lenovo, taking the "Le" from Legend and adding "novo", the Latin word for "new", to reflect the spirit of innovation at the core of the company. The company name was also changed into Lenovo in the following year. [clii]

In 2004, Lenovo announced the acquisition of IBM's Personal Computing Division with a total of 12.5 billion US dollar (6.5 billion of cash & 6 billion worth of Lenovo's stock). The acquisition was completed in 2005 enabling Lenovo to jump from the ninth to the third-largest personal computer company in the world that closely followed Dell and Phillip. [cliii]

THE IBM PC DIVISION ACQUISITION

IBM's motivations for spinning off its PC division were clear: the division recorded a net loss of $258 million in 2003 and $171 million in 2002 and had required a total parent company equity infusion totalling $987 million as of June 2004. In addition, the division was an "orphan" within the organization, as it did not fit within IBM's broader strategy to focus on higher margin enterprise and services businesses. [cliv] In the summer of 2002, IBM's then chief financial officer, John R. Joyce, offered to sell the company's struggling PC business to Legend. But IBM's PC unit had lost nearly $400 million the previous year. At that time, Legend executives declined the deal. [clv]

In 2004, Lenovo was hungry to become a global player. Once again, the IBM PC division was offered to Lenovo. When Lenovo's CFO Ma took her first trip to New York to talk things over with IBM negotiator Peter Lynt, she saw that IBM had radically restructured the PC unit and that costs had been slashed. She was astonished by the numbers and became an advocate for the acquisition. [clvi]

In acquiring the IBM PC Division, Lenovo's main motives were:
- to enable it to transform itself into a global multinational corporation;
- to lower the cost of production by M&A with IBM that could enable Lenovo to learn the supply-chain management from IBM;
- to acquire an international brand from IBM;
- to have access to new customers;
- to expand the company's structure in order to strengthen its bargaining position with its supplier. [clvii]

Being largely a localized company, Lenovo's sales and growth levels had reached maturity in the past few years. The acquisition was necessary and was the fastest way for the company to reach other markets in order to increase its sales and continue expanding. In China, Lenovo's market share in the local market had shrunk due to a decrease in sales demand. PC suppliers had adopted a price competition strategy to stabilize its market share. At the same time China opened up for PC giants such as Dell, Phillip and IBM. Lenovo was facing strong competitive pressure from both multinational and local suppliers. International expansion was an essential stepping-stone for growth. [clviii]

Access to technology and research and development skills within IBM was another motivating factor for the acquisition. To Lenovo, it meant that if it was able to integrate successfully with IBM in terms of development skills and supplier-chain management, the company would be a large integrated PC company, able to engage in R&D, production, manufacturing, distribution, marketing, and after-sales-service. Lenovo would be able to achieve a potential competitive advantage through reduced costs of production. [clix]

The agreement enabling Lenovo to use the international brand, ThinkPad, for five years was another important motive. Acquiring a well known international company would allow Lenovo to use the brand of the acquired company in the first stage of introducing its products to the international market and might increase the willingness of customers to try their products. China's products had been marketed as low quality and less expensive products. Using a well-known brand such as IBM could improve the impression of customers towards the product, enabling Lenovo to market its product at the higher end of the market. [clx]

As stated earlier, Lenovo had reached its peak in its sales in the local markets and hardly moved further. Lenovo had attempted to diversify itself from main PC producer to IT service consultation but with no success. With the acquisition of the IBM PC-department, Lenovo reset its strategic focus on its PC production, use of the international brands like ThinkPad for five years trusting that it could reach more new customers through international expansion. [clxi]

It was also expected that once the acquisition made Lenovo the third largest leading PC producer in the world, the huge increase in the size of the company after the M&A would put Lenovo in a better bargaining position with its suppliers. [clxii]

The parties estimated that Lenovo- IBM's scale would create cost synergies of $150-200 million a year on procurement savings alone. [clxiii]

In forging a deal, IBM and Lenovo agreed that it would not be a simple acquisition of assets. Rather, it would be a strategic alliance. Among the agreements reached were that: IBM would sell Lenovo PCs through its sales force and distribution network, IBM would provide services and financing for Lenovo PCs -- and allow Lenovo to use the vaunted IBM brand name for five years. In turn, Lenovo, which is still partly owned by the government's Chinese Academy of Sciences, would help IBM gain entrée into the promising China market. [clxiv]

INTEGRATION CHALLENGES

The Lenovo-IBM PC transaction was fraught with cultural and operational integration risks. Cultural and operational integration challenges were significant. The two companies had distinct cultures: IBM PC was an established global business with a Western management mindset, whereas Lenovo was a purely China-focused company run by local Chinese entrepreneurs. Further, Lenovo's management had very limited experience operating outside China and there was a risk that the key US management needed to run the international portion of the combined business would leave because of potential cultural clashes. [clxv]

As for operational risks, it was recognized that it would not be an easy task to subsume a global icon operating in 160 countries within a company one third its size and that which operates in only one country. Both, the challenge of combining the two businesses in their current format as well as the planned restructuring of the supply chain and manufacturing added significantly to that risk. In particular, successfully executing two major cost initiatives fundamental to the industrial logic of the acquisition was far from assured. The PC division had been posting a loss. Achieving preferential terms from suppliers and fully leveraging Lenovo's low cost infrastructure to reduce the global operating costs were very ambitious goals that had never before been attempted by a Chinese company. At that time, no Chinese company had yet successfully turned around a loss-making company into a profit-making company. [clxvi]

As for cultural integration, even during the early stages of the acquisition, the issue of Lenovo's corporate culture had already been raised. One writer asked, "Can a company molded in the tradition of socialist state-owned enterprises, and which still holds twice-daily exercise sessions and company sing-alongs, transform itself into a global computer powerhouse?" [clxvii]

Duncan Clark, a managing director of BDA China Ltd., a Beijing-based consulting firm, observed that, "The cultural challenges are going to be big. (Lenovo is) traditional, in the state-owned enterprise style. Lenovo hasn't had a particularly successful track record of partnerships with foreign companies." [clxviii]

The same article recounted that in 2002, Lenovo went to Silicon Valley to recruit middle managers. A handful of U.S.- educated Chinese were hired, most of them taking huge pay cuts for the excitement of working for a Chinese company with worldwide ambitions. But about a year later, almost all of them had quit. A U.S.- educated Chinese man who worked at Lenovo for a little more than a year, described its culture as very Chinese and so strange, that most employees who had been educated abroad soon left. [clxix]

For instance, twice a day, the sound system broadcasted throughout the company's headquarters in northwestern Beijing, a song formally known as the Number Six Broadcast Exercises, a set of gentle stretches and knee-bends that any child who had grown up in communist China has learned. Participation is voluntary but highly encouraged. [clxx]

Another quirky custom was to encourage people who were late for meetings to stand behind their chair for the first minute to humiliate them into being punctual in the future. Employees' time is strictly monitored. Card keys allow the company to keep track of when the employees are in the building. Time spent outside the building during work hours had to be accounted for and if no reasonable explanation was given, a deduction could be made from an employee's paycheck. Lenovo also has a company song that is played in the building every morning at 8a.m. and is sung by workers at the start of company-wide meetings. [clxxi]

The strict discipline was likely due to the initiative of the Lenovo chairman and co-founder Liu Chuanzi, who has a military background. "It's very militaristic," the former employee said. "It's not an environment that fosters creativity. You just have to do what you're told." [clxxii]

At the time of the acquisition, the vast majority of the staff were young and had worked only at Lenovo since graduating from college. Few spoke English and many had never even met a foreigner. Almost no managers had any international business experience, and overseas training, common at multinational companies ,was non-existent in China. [clxxiii]

In other words, at the time of the acquisition, the cultural issues that Lenovo had to hurdle were numerous. The cultural issues stemmed not just from differences in corporate culture but also in the national cultures.
IMPACT OF DIFFERENT NATIONAL CULTURES

Sharona Peng used the integration efforts of Lenovo – IBM PC Division transaction as a subject for her masteral thesis in Auckland University. In her thesis, she reviewed the national cultural attitudes of China and the United States since this was also important in examining corporate culture; she examined the stages of integration and then interviewed various managers and key employees in Lenovo to determine the success of its cross-cultural and management integration. [clxxiv]

Citing Hofstede, Peng stated that, Chinese culture attitudes are characterized by high-power distance, collectivism, masculinity and high-uncertainty avoidance. [clxxv]

In relation to those culture attitudes, she examined an important Chinese cultural concept: "guanxi".

Guanxi is the granting of preferential treatment to business partners in exchange for favours and obligations. It requires reciprocity and obligation to return a favor. If the obligation is not fulfilled within a short period of time, social harmony between managers may be disturbed as the non-reciprocity will have caused them to lose face. Guanxi networks are considered to be essential for doing business in China. Business in China cannot be conducted while keeping guanxi at bay as personal contacts play an essential role in the Chinese way of doing business. [clxxvi]

Many foreign firms have learned that guanxi means developing good relationships with local government officials. That would include personal contact, gift exchanges and never doing anything that would cause the Chinese to lose face. While it is seen as an essential factor for Chinese people, it can be seen as a slow and often frustrating process from a Westerner's perspective. [clxxvii]

Power distance, a key component of Chinese national culture, is the expectation that power is distributed unequally. This can be seen in China's pervasive centralized authority and hierarchical structures. The Chinese expect power to be unequally distributed and naturally defer to their perceived superiors whom they expect to be benevolent and to treat all people fairly, providing them with stability, close supervision and explicit rules. In nations characterized by high power distance like China, organizational structures generally work best if they are formal and hierarchical. Those in subordinate positions expect the more powerful-high-ranking individuals to take responsibility for decision making. Power distance is consistent with the focus on guanxi relationships with upper-level authorities particularly in state-owned enterprise and the strong hierarchical ordering that makes empowerment challenging. [clxxviii]

Chinese national culture is also highly collective. It is characterized by a preference for a tightly knit social network, an expectation that in-group members will support each other and a strong urge to maintain social harmony and interdependence within the in-group. Collectivism refers to the degree to which the society emphasizes the role of the individual versus the role of the group. Nations with high collectivism are likely to show an emotional attachment to organizations and to emphasize on "we are greater as a group." [clxxix]

Chinese society is also characterized as masculine. Peng cites Hofstede, who states that, "a society is called masculine when emotional gender roles are clearly distinct: men are supposed to be assertive, tough, and focused on material success, whereas women are supposed to be more modest, tender, and concerned with the quality of life". Boys are socialized towards assertiveness, ambition and competition and are expected to aspire for career advancement while girls are polarized between those who want a career and the majority who don't. The resolution of conflicts in this culture society is "letting the best men win". Organizations in masculine society stress the result and reward on the basis of equity, rewarding everyone on the

41

basis of performance accordingly. In addition, as the work ethos for the society is "live to work," more money is preferable to more leisure time. [clxxx]

China is seen as a high-uncertainty avoidance culture. High-uncertainty avoidance is defined as the extent to which the members of a culture feel threatened by an ambiguous or unknown (unfamiliar) situation. It is expressed through nervous stress and a need for predictability through written and unwritten rules. [clxxxi]

It is different from risk avoidance in the sense that risk is expressed as a percentage of probability that a particular event may happen, whereas uncertainty has no probability attached to it. Consequently, in this situation it is expected that anything can occur. It is said that in a high-uncertainty avoidance society, the level of stress is considered to be high as people believe that "the uncertainty inherent in life is a continuous threat that must be fought". Also, as the emotional need for rules in a high-uncertainty avoidance culture is strong, people have been programmed since their early childhood to feel comfortable in structured environment. [clxxxii]

People in this society have more formal laws and informal rules controlling the rights and duties of employers and employees. They also have more internal regulations controlling work processes. This can lead to rule-oriented behaviour that are purely ritual, inconsistent or even dysfunctional and therefore problems can arise even if people may not realize ineffective rules can also satisfy people's emotional needs in this society. Moreover, there is a strong belief in expertise on the work floor and specialists and organizations are often likely to reward "intrapreneurs" (those who are highly innovative, a risk taker and given much freedom to develop products or subsidiary businesses in a company). Thus, people in high- uncertainty avoidance culture can be less creative and innovative as compared to low-uncertainty culture. [clxxxiii]

On the other hand, the culture of United States has been described as low-power distance, individualism, and low-uncertainty avoidance. [clxxxiv]

In a low-power distance culture, subordinates and superiors treat each other as equal in contrast to an hierarchical system that is typified by an inequality of roles. In this culture, organizations are decentralized, with relatively flat hierarchical pyramids and limited numbers of supervisory personnel. Salary ranges between top and bottom job are relatively small; workers are highly qualified and highly-skilled and manual work has a higher status than low-skilled office work. Privileges for higher-ups are considered undesirable so that all should use the same parking space, toilets and cafeteria. Moreover, superiors should be accessible to subordinates and the ideal boss is a resourceful democrat. Subordinates are expected to be consulted before a decision is made that affects their work, but they accept that the boss is the final decision-maker. Organizations in this society tend to be more likely to have structured ways of dealing with employee complaints on alleged power abuses. [clxxxv]

Where China is seen as a collective society, the culture of the United States is characterized by individualism. Citing Hofstede, Peng states that individualism is defined as "loose ties between individuals," meaning everyone in the society is expected to look after him or herself and his or her immediate family. [clxxxvi]

Employees are expected to act according to their own interest but in a manner that their self-interest and that of the employer's coincide. In addition, family relationships are often dismissed as undesirable in the hiring process as they may lead to nepotism and conflicts of interest.

Thus, in some companies if one employee marries another, one of them would have to leave the company. [clxxxvii]

The relationship between employer and employee is primarily conceived as a business transaction, a calculative relationship between buyers and sellers in a labor market such that an employee's poor performance as a reason to terminate a work relationship or a better pay offer from another employer are legitimate and socially acceptable. Furthermore, management in an individualist society is, in essence, management of individuals. Subordinates can usually be moved around individually. It is expected that if there are any incentives or bonus to be given, it should link to the individual's performance. [clxxxviii]

The United States is seen as a feminine society. A society is feminine when emotional gender roles overlap: both men and women are supposed to be modest, tender and concerned with the quality of life. In a workplace where the culture is feminine, there is a preference for resolving conflicts by compromise and negotiation. While there may occasionally be some verbal insult, both between bosses and subordinates, yet there is a "sense of moderation" that enables both parties to continue working together. Also, there are large possibilities open for women managers. And organizations in feminine societies are more likely to reward people on the basis of equality rather than equity. As for work ethos, the emphasis is on "work to live". Careers are considered optional for both genders and more leisure time would be preferable over more money. Consequently, the concept of "work-life balance" seems to be more important for people in feminine society as compared to masculine one. [clxxxix]

Americans, as opposed to the Chinese, have low uncertainty avoidance. In countries with weak uncertainty avoidance, people can display an emotional horror of formal rules as they believe that rules should only be established in the case of absolute necessity such as determining whether the traffic should be kept left or right. Low-uncertainty avoidance cultures have strong belief in common sense and gonoralism. For example, people in this society often believe that "a study at a good university is a valid entry ticket for a business management career." Moreover, they are relatively free from rules and thus better at invention but worse at implementation, as opposed to people in strong certainty avoidance culture. [cxc]

The foregoing discussion shows that China and United States have cultural characteristics that are poles apart from each other, a situation that may pose difficulties for an organization that needs to develop management techniques and training packages for its employees. For instance, a standard element in the training of first-line managers is how to conduct appraisal interviews with their subordinates in which individual's performance is reviewed and discussed between managers and subordinates. For conducting performance appraisals and the ability to communicate bad news are thought of as a key skill for a successful manager. However, in a collective society, discussing a person's performance openly with him or her is likely to clash head-on with society's harmony norm and may be felt by the subordinate as an unacceptable loss of face. [cxci]

In one study, an analyst found that national difference in beliefs regarding organization practices is considerably greater in multi-national firms than in single national samples. The author of the study suggests that the deeper level of underlying assumptions is derived from one's national culture, it is therefore expected that national culture constitutes a crucial factor in M&A conflicts in its quest for successful integration. His results led another analyst to suggest that national culture may play a stronger role in the face of a strong corporate culture. However, another author suggests that while national culture forms one's values through early socialization, corporate culture involves the subsequent acquisition of organization practices and symbols in the firm. Thus, he proposes that national and corporate cultures are distinctive but related. In that sense, there is no reason to believe that the impact of national culture's clash will not be equal, if not greater than the one produced by corporate culture. [cxcii]

LENOVO'S CULTURAL INTEGRATION INITIATIVES

From the onset, Lenovo recognized the enormous challenges that it faced because of the difference not only in corporate but also in national cultures. Among its first moves was to agree to move its headquarters to a more global location (New York) and to adopt English as the official language of the corporation. The former head of the IBM PC Divisions, Stephen Ward became the first CEO of the new Lenovo. The former CEO of Lenovo, Yuanqing Yang, moved to the US and learnt English. [cxciii]

To bridge the gap between eastern and western cultures, the company conducted a "cultural audit" of its employees, discovering that former IBM-ers didn't fully trust the new owners and that original Lenovo workers felt their new American brethren were a bit undisciplined—let off the hook too frequently for blown deadlines or missed targets. Part of the problem was basic communication--westerners tend to speak first, then listen, and easterners tend to listen, then speak. The human resources manager counselled Americans to slow down when they talk and Asians to be more outspoken. [cxciv]

Prior to the acquisition, Lenovo anticipated that its biggest challenge would be how to manage its people. Among its main concerns was how to prevent IBM employee turnover. Since IBM employees were very proud of being part of IBM, the question was whether they would be willing to accept the new company structure and choose to stay with Lenovo. [cxcv]

To avert this problem, even before the acquisition was completed, Lenovo conducted a survey within Lenovo as well as in IBM's PC department to find out staff opinion towards the M&A. Results showed that on the whole, Lenovo staff was positive about the M&A as they believed that the integration would advance the company to an international level. With respect to the IBM PC department staff, survey results revealed that a majority were willing to stay with the new company after acquisition, especially when it appeared that Lenovo would manage the company in an international manner and guarantee their remuneration schemes and welfare. [cxcvi]

Lenovo also anticipated challenges in managing and integrating the culture of Lenovo and the IBM PC Division. Lenovo was faced not only with the challenge of integrating two corporate cultures, but also two national cultures - West and East, which was more difficult as the national culture is deeply rooted in people's life. [cxcvii]

At, the pre-planning stage, Lenovo designed a range of strategy such as cocktail parties, a culture integration discussion board, setting up a cultural integration committee to integrate two teams as well as to encourage communication between them. [cxcviii]

However, Lenovo did not plan to integrate the management system of the IBM PC department in the first phase of the M&A, choosing instead to manage two teams separately to prevent conflict from arising in the first phase. Lenovo did not implement new management systems after the acquisition, neither did it try to adjust and make IBM's management system look like Lenovo's.

Instead, a separate management style was adopted by the company in which each team had its own management procedures for managing the staff. There were plans, though, to design a new management system, picking all the strengths from each team that would enable the company to achieve a better position and obtain the competitive advantage. [cxcix]

With respect to differences in salary, Lenovo had guaranteed the remuneration system of IBM would remain intact. So therefore, even if Lenovo's salary system was based on a lower fixed salary and high in bonus/commissions whereas IBM was focused on high salaries and low bonuses/commissions, Lenovo had to adjust the remuneration system for the Lenovo staff to balance with what employees of IBM PC-D received. [cc]

With respect to communications, both teams (Lenovo and IBM PC division) adopted a triangular information flow method whereby senior management teams passed down information to managers of each department and department managers in turn would pass information to subordinates. To reduce ambiguities and also for purposes of establishing an audit trail, email became the main medium for communication. Employees emailed one another for day-to-day operational issues and senior teams sent announcements or staff newsletters through email on a monthly basis. [cci]

Some employees also voluntarily took part in a cultural integration committee to help employees to become more culturally aware and encourage communication between two teams. Employees from various departments including IBM PC department who were members of the committee met on a regular basis to design and organize functions and activities to encourage interaction between the teams. Initiatives organized by the committee to encourage interactions included staff discussion forums, cocktail parties, monthly newsletters. They also selected a most culturally aware employee of the month. [ccii]

Staff discussion forums were designed to encourage staff to clear the air due to corporate or national culture issues and to make suggestions to solve the problems on an individual/company basis. Topics were posted in the discussion forums to encourage interaction. Staff from Lenovo, IBM PC-D as well as western employees from international branches actively participated in the discussion forum by posting questions and comments on the discussion forum. [cciii]

A cocktail party was also held on a regular basis, aiming to encourage interaction between employees. A bilingual approach was adopted in which one host spoke Chinese and another spoke English. It would begin with a report from the cultural integration committee on the integration process in terms of employee interaction. After that a reward would be given to an employee of the month who is deemed to have made the best contribution in helping staff become culturally aware. [cciv]

Criteria for selection included contributing topics and actively participating in the discussion forums. Aside from being rewarded during the cocktail party, the selected candidate would be mentioned in the monthly newsletter. This form of recognition was meant to motivate them to understand the culture of others.

After announcing the reward, the staff would be free to talk with each other while free drinks and food would be provided by the company. [ccv]

45

In the staff monthly newsletter, a special section called "Culture Discovery", a member of the senior management team would discuss how to effectively integrate Lenovo and IBM by tackling culture difference problems. In the September 2006 issue, the then chair of Lenovo, Yuanquing Yang, discussed the company's first culture integration strategy which focused on core values, management system and national differences between western and Asian employees. [ccvi]

RESULTS OF THE INTEGRATION INITIATIVES

According to the study conducted by Peng, culture clashes were not too severe. In fact, there were some participants who cited benefits arising from the acquisition such as increased opportunities and training for employees in the China region because of classes to improve their English and increase cultural awareness or, as in the case of a Chinese secretary, the redefining of job tasks. In her perception, her job became more professional because from the Chinese perspective, a secretary is supposed to smoothen the job of the manager. However, from the western point of view, a secretary would be focused on the job tasks within the organization rather than on the manager. [ccvii]

Conflicts that did arise were minor and were dealt with. Among those Peng cited were as follows:

1. The problem with the office chairs – IBM PC Division people brought in their own chairs which were of better quality than those of Lenovo. To solve the conflict, Lenovo standardized all furniture in the office;

2. Welfare benefits – instead of adjusting the benefits of the IBM team, Lenovo made incremental changes for the Lenovo team to balance things off;

3. More China based staff worked overtime because of web meetings with colleagues from America. Many of them believed that working over-time is essential. Subordinates were not expected to leave the office before the manager. This may be related to the national culture attitudes characterized by Chinese culture of high-power distance and Confucianism in which high-rank individuals are always respected by subordinates. Staff in the China region chose to compromise.

4. Different attitudes displayed by Chinese and Westerners during meetings: Chinese colleagues were more likely to listen to others and less likely to express his/her personal opinions or ask questions, whereas Western employees were more likely to actively interact with others during meetings. As a result, Western employees were mostly dominant in meetings and most Western employees believed Chinese employees were shy. Peng explains that such behaviour could be traced back to Chinese education whereby students are expected to focus and listen to what the teacher has taught and refrain from asking questions during class time. To address this problem, Lenovo organized functions or activities to encourage communication between two teams and awareness of culture differences between each other.

5. Introducing Chinese culture to foreign colleagues: In one instance, a Western Lenovo staff member who had already been working for them for three months suddenly questioned a Chinese employee about the company's practice of playing 20 year old music in the morning and music for radio gymnastic exercises in the mid- morning and mid -afternoon. The other employee informed him that it was their (Chinese) culture and

that they had done exercise with this kind of music since they were young. But what surprised the employee was that a foreign colleague who had been with them every day for three months knew nothing about what they were used to. [ccviii]

ANALYSIS OF THE INTEGRATION INITIATIVES

Lenovo adopted a separation mode of integration allowing IBM PC-D to preserve their own culture and practices by keeping it separate from and independent of the dominant group. As a result, IBM PC-D functioned as a separate unit under the financial umbrella of the parent company. Lenovo chose the separation mode of integration but took many initiatives in encouraging two teams to interact and communicate with each other. Also, when differences with IBM PC-D arose, Lenovo chose to accommodate it in resolving problems. [ccix]

In Peng's analysis, Lenovo chose the separate mode of integration because Lenovo did not find it necessary to integrate for various reasons such as similarity in core values,, the need to ensure smooth operations worldwide and its main aim to gain access to technology. [ccx]

Instead of devising a new system to integrate Lenovo and IBM PC-D, Lenovo used the culture integration committee as an intermediary to transfer information to both teams. Without integrating the two teams as a whole, members of both teams were less likely to have a lot of opportunities to contact each other apart from the activities such as the cocktail party, and staff discussion forum which were organized by the culture integration committee. [ccxi]

On the other hand, Peng found that there were not many conflicts in culture. And when a problem would arise, the response of Lenovo employees would be one of accommodation. She stated that, "On one hand, as guanxi puts emphasis on maintaining good relationship with others, the Chinese employees are less likely to reject and instead try to accommodate to others as a favour in order to prevent conflicts from arising. On the other hand, Confucianism values' accepting others, especially when one is a host. Therefore, in the case of Lenovo, Chinese employees regarded themselves as the host and senior members of the organization. It is therefore sensible that they should accommodate themselves to the team of IBM PC-D as they treated members of IBM PC-D as new members of the organization and had to maintain good relationship with the new colleagues by being friendly and cooperative." [ccxii]

She noted, however, that an accommodation strategy in resolving problems could lead to poor work-life balance for its Chinese employees. For example, many Chinese employees would have to work overtime in order to attend web meetings with its US colleagues. Their unbalanced life style was likely to lead to stress and harm their health. Ultimately, that could further hinder the operation efficiency of the organization. [ccxiii]

DID THE INTEGRATION INITIATIVES WORK?

Peng concluded that as of the time of the writing of her paper, the integration stage of Lenovo was still in the conflict stage. [ccxiv] If that were the case, then it could not be said that the initiatives did work. However, she did note that culture conflicts were minor in nature and those that did arise were resolved through accommodation.

In 2007, one writer concluded that the integration process was successful. [ccxv]

However, by 2009, the corporation had faltered necessitating organizational changes. It announced its plan to cut 11 percent of its workforce, or 2,500 jobs worldwide, and to reduce executive compensations by 30 percent to 50 percent as part of measures to counter declining profits amidst the global recession. It also planned to merge its China and Asia Pacific operations to reduce expenses. [ccxvi]

Lenovo had successfully stopped the losses in IBM's prestigious but long-time bleeding PC business and risen from a domestic PC maker to one of China's most international companies. But the success did not make Lenovo immune from the slowing IT demand amid the global economic crisis. In 2008, Lenovo's profits in its second quarter plunged 78 percent because of sluggish demands in the corporate sector (corporate entities buy 60 to 70 percent of its products) and slower business in China. Its share in the global PC market also dropped to 7.7 percent in the third quarter ending December from 8.2 percent a year earlier, according to research firm IDC. [ccxvii]

According to one expert, Lenovo's problem lay in its inability to copy its success in China to other markets. Other experts stated that it was because Lenovo had made many compromises after acquiring IBM's PC business that it gave up some of its Chinese identity, increased its difficulty in expanding its successful Chinese experience to other markets and increased the culture conflicts between its Chinese employees and foreign executives. [ccxviii]

In their restructuring plan, the two separated Asia Pacific and Greater China regions were merged into a single operation under Chen Shaopeng, Lenovo's former head of Greater China and Russia, and Lenovo's most successful market region. The company also moved the Asia Pacific headquarters from Singapore to Beijing. An analyst stated that the restructuring plan reflected its efforts to increase the role of its Chinese operations in the international markets where Lenovo could generate more revenue. [ccxix]

After four years on the sidelines, Liu Chuanzhi took back control of Lenovo's management from its command-control American CEO and recast Lenovo as a global company with a consensus-style Chinese management structure. [ccxx]

Lenovo required fundamental reform. Factions had formed in the company's top echelons — the original Chinese managers, the IBM old guard and new executives imported by Amelio (Lenovo's last American CEO) — which loosened the team's cohesion. His biggest concern, however, was that the rapid changes Lenovo had made in its culture after the IBM acquisition were undermining the effectiveness of its management. He believed Lenovo had to get back to its roots or to the "Lenovo way" — the culture that had been such an important part of Lenovo's success. [ccxxi]

The "Lenovo way" is based on a collective decision making process in which the CEO develops and implements strategy as part of tight-knit group of executives. Liu contrasts the Lenovo way with what he sees as the "classic MBA way," where a dominant CEO makes decisions more independently and then works with the individual chiefs of the business units to execute them. [ccxxii]

Liu states that it is a home grown system forged over his years by the trials of building Lenovo. It is not culturally Chinese, although consensus-based management processes are common in many Asian firms. He sees it as an alternative to Western management practices

— perhaps one better suited to certain cases, like Lenovo's, in which the management team is Sino-global. He states that the Lenovo way of decision making is more prudent and more thorough. [ccxxiii]

Liu states that the former CEO Amelio's approach was the classic methodology in MBA textbooks. However, Amelio was facing a very complicated situation where there are different teams from different cultures and nations. It was very hard to really mobilize or motivate [these] teams to achieve goals using the classic method. [ccxxiv]

Liu narrowed the senior management team down to an eight-member executive committee that meets regularly to discuss strategy and carefully plan its execution. [ccxxv]

Schuman states that Liu's new management structure seems to have energized Lenovo — although a rebounding economy didn't hurt either. The rebound shows in a number of initiatives – re-acquisition of a handset maker, development of new products. [ccxxvi] Also, the company returned to profitability in the second half of 2009, and it is aggressively pushing into emerging markets, where, by using its experience in China, managers believe they might hold a special advantage. Lenovo's PC shipments surged 58% last quarter from the same period a year earlier, while the total market grew 24%. [ccxxvii]

THE FUTURE

In 2005, Chinese media had questioned the Lenovo – IBM PC division deal, many likening it to a snake swallowing an elephant. "Will Lenovo become an elephant or have a bad case of indigestion?" asked the Yangcheng Evening News, a major paper in southern China. "Only time will tell." [ccxxviii]

Liu said, however, to come back after more results to say that the Lenovo way works. [ccxxix]

China is now the second largest economy in the world, having just recently dislodged Japan. China based corporations are now investing globally for various reasons such as a need to tap oil and other mineral resources or to tap ever growing markets or to acquire new brands. The latest acquisition is the acquisition of Volvo by automaker Zhejiang Geely Holding Group.

Will the Lenovo way transform its acquisition of the IBM-PC division into a success such that Lenovo would regain its status as one of the top three PC makers in the market?

Will the Lenovo way which Liu wishes to share with other corporations assist ambitious China corporations successfully grow through the strategy of M & A's?
Only time will tell. From what we see so far, things look upbeat.

Endnotes

_____

[ii] *Ravenscraft and Scherer.* 1987; *Farlex Financial Dictionary , 2009 ; Collins English Dictionary and Thesaurus 2006; Webster's New World College Dictionary Copyright © 2010;* Dr. Michael Teng, *Fundamentals of Buying a Business;* David L. Scott, *"Wall Street Words: An A to Z Guide to Investment Terms for Today's Investor,"* 2003 by Houghton Mifflin Company; *"Investor Dictionary"* http://www.investordictionary.com/definition/reverse+merger.aspx; *Economy watch,* http://www.economywatch.com/mergers-acquisitions/type/extension-merger-product-extension.html; *Securities Law Institute* http://www.securitieslawinstitute.com/m&a.html#triangular%20merger

[iii] Ganesh Chand, "Perspectives on Mergers & Acquisitions*," Mergers & Acquisitions: Issues and Perspectives from the Asia Pacific Region,* Asian Productivity Organization, 2009, ISBN: 92-833-7031-3. http://www.apo-tokyo.org/00e-books/IS-38_M&A.htm

[iv] See note i.

[v] Moon Jyun-Kim, "Trends and Practices in the Global Markets*," Mergers & Acquisitions: Issues and Perspectives from the Asia Pacific Region,* Asian Productivity Organization, 2009, ISBN: 92-833-7031-3. http://www.apo-tokyo.org/00e-books/IS-38_M&A.htm

[vi] *Wordnet search,* http://wordnetweb.princeton.edu/perl/webwn?s=oligopoly

[vii] Moon Jyun-Kim, "Trends and Practices in the Global Markets," *Mergers & Acquisitions: Issues and Perspectives from the Asia Pacific Region,* Asian Productivity Organization, 2009, ISBN: 92-833-7031-3. http://www.apo-tokyo.org/00e-books/IS-38_M&A.htm

[viii] See Moon Jyun-Kim, Note vi.

[ix] Marv Dumon, *"The Buy-Side Of The M&A Process,"* ,http://www.investopedia.com/articles/stocks/07/buyside_m_and_a.asp; Oliver Recklies, *"Vision as Key Factor in Merger Processes",* (2001) *http://www.themanager.org/strategy/Merger_Vision.htm* ; .Bizmove.com, *"Buy and Sell Business: How to Buy Business",* http://www.bizmove.com/buying/m5a.htm; William R. Pursche, *"Building Better Bids"* 1988, http://www.firstcalladvisors.com/files/BuildingBetterBidsV2.pdf.

[x] See Note iii.

[xi] Christopher Kummer, "Overcoming the Challenges and Issues of Post-Merger Integration," *Mergers & Acquisitions: Issues and Perspectives from the Asia Pacific Region,* Asian Productivity Organization, 2009, ISBN: 92-833-7031-3. http://www.apo-tokyo.org/00e-books/IS-38_M&A.htm

[xii] Marv Dumon, *"The Buy-Side Of The M&A Process,"* http://www.investopedia.com/articles/stocks/07/buyside m and a.asp

[xiii] Marv Dumon, *"The Buy-Side Of The M&A Process,"* ,http://www.investopedia.com/articles/stocks/07/buyside m and a.asp

[xiv] Nils Bohlin, Eliot Daley, and Sue Thomson, "Successful Post-Merger Integration: Realizing the Synergies." http://www.manda-institute.org/docs/m&a/adlittle 02 Successful%20Post-Merger%20Integration%20-%20Realising%20the%20Synergies.pdf

[xv] Oliver Recklies, *"Vision as Key Factor in Merger Processes"*, 2001, http://www.themanager.org/strategy/Merger Vision.htm.

[xvi] *Investopedia,* *http://vsc.biz/public/business/businessfocus/library/business_valuation_methods.pdf* *Investopedia;* Business Dictionary.com, *http://www.businessdictionary.com/definition/asset-valuation.html;* Small *Business Encyclopedia: http://www.referenceforbusiness.com/small/Sm-Z/Valuation.html;* David Bird, *Business Valuation Methods,* 2007, *http://vsc.biz/public/business/businessfocus/library/business valuation methods.pdf*

[xvii] See note xv

[xviii] See note xv

[xix] See note xv

[xx] Ventureline, ACCOUNTING TERMS - ACCOUNTING DICTIONARY - ACCOUNTING GLOSSARY - http://www.ventureline.com/accounting-glossary/C/capitalization-of-maintainable-earnings-definition/

[xxi] See note xix

[xxii] See note xix

[xxiii] See note xix

[xxiv] David Bird, *Business Valuation Methods,* 2007, *http://vsc.biz/public/business/businessfocus/library/business valuation methods.pdf*

[xxv] See note xiv

[xxvi] Prof. Ian Giddy "Mergers & Acquisitions: An Introduction," New York University, 2006, http://pages.stern.nyu.edu/~igiddy/articles/mergers intro.htm; Dr. Michael Teng, *Fundamentals of Buying a Business* *(e-book);* Marv Dumon, *"The Buy-Side Of The M&A Process,"* ,http://www.investopedia.com/articles/stocks/07/buyside m and a.asp

[xxvii] Foreword, *Mergers & Acquisitions: Issues and Perspectives from the Asia Pacific Region,* Asian Productivity Organization, 2009, ISBN: 92-833-7031-3. http://www.apo-tokyo.org/00e-books/IS-38_M&A.htm

[xxviii] Albert J. Viscio, John R. Harbison, Amy Asin and Richard P. Vitaro, "Post-Merger Integration: What Makes Mergers Work?," *Strategy + Business,* 4th Quarter, 1999. Reprint No. 99404. http://www.strategy-business.com/article/13903?gko=975a6

[xxix] J. P. Chevriere, "Rules for the road in post-merger integration," 1999. http://www.offshore-mag.com/index/article-display/24799/articles/offshore/volume-59/issue-1/news/general-interest/rules-for-the-road-in-post-merger-integration.html

[xxx] See J. P. Chevriere, note xxix.

[xxxi] *Fazilah Abdul Samad,* "Malaysian Best Practice for Cross-Border Acquisition", *Mergers & Acquisitions: Issues and Perspectives from the Asia Pacific Region,* Asian Productivity Organization, 2009, ISBN: 92-833-7031-3. http://www.apo-tokyo.org/00e-books/IS-38_M&A.htm

[xxxii] Bill Pursche, Putting the "Art" Back into Post Merger Integration, 2000, BillPursche@FirstCallAdvisors.com

[xxxiii] Aralanta M (2005) " Evaluating Success in Post-merger IS Integration: A Case Study," *The Electronic Journal Information Systems Evaluation* Volume 8 Issue 3, pp 143-150, available online at www.ejise.com

[xxxiv] Christopher Kummer, "Overcoming the Challenges and Issues of Post-Merger Integration," *Mergers & Acquisitions: Issues and Perspectives from the Asia Pacific Region,* Asian Productivity Organization, 2009, ISBN: 92-833-7031-3. http://www.apo-tokyo.org/00e-books/IS-38_M&A.htm

[xxxv] H. Donald Hopkins, "Cross-Border Mergers and Acquisitions: Do Strategy or Post-Merger Integration Matter?" *International Management Review,* Vol. 4 No. 1 2008, http://www.usimr.org/IMR-1-2008/v4n108-art1.pdf

[xxxvi] See Kummer, Note xxxiv, citing Chatterjee, Lubatkin, Schweiger & Weber, 1992.

[xxxvii] See Kummer, Note xxxiv, citing Michael Porter, 1991.

[xxxviii] Wordnet, a lexical database for English, *wordnetweb.princeton.edu/perl/webwn*; Wikipedia, citing Anthony F., Buono; Bowditch, James L (1989). *The human side of mergers and acquisitions: Managing collisions between people, cultures, and organizations.* San Francisco: Jossey-Bass Publishers. ISBN 1555421350.

[xxxix] Yinmei Wan, "*Managing Post-Merger Integration: A Case Study of a Merger in Chinese Higher Education,*" Doctoral Dissertation for University of Michigan, 2008 citing *Birkinshaw, Bresman, & Hakanson,* (2000); *Shrivastava*, (1986); *Waldman* (2004), http://deepblue.lib.umich.edu/handle/2027.42/58541

[xl] Johannes Gerds and Freddy Strottmann with Pakshalika Jayaprakash, "Post Merger Integration: Hard Data, Hard Truths," *DeLoitte Review*, Issue 6 (2010)

[xli] See note xxxix, Yinmei Wan, citing *Birkinshaw, Bresman, & Hakanson,* (2000); *Shrivastava*, (1986); *Waldman* (2004).

[xlii] See note xxxix, Yinmei Wan citing Shrivastava (1986).

[xliii] See note xxxixYinmei Wan summarizing Shrivastava (1986)

[xliv] See note xxxix, Yinmei Wan summarizing Birkinshaw, Bresman & Hakanson (2000).

[xlv] H. Donald Hopkins, "Cross-Border Mergers and Acquisitions: Do Strategy or Post-Merger Integration Matter?" *International Management Review,* Vol. 4 No. 1 2008, http://www.usimr.org/IMR-1-2008/v4n108-art1.pdf

[xlvi] See note xxxiv, Christopher Kummer.

[xlvii] See xxxiv, Christopher Kummer.

[xlviii] SANDY WEINER AND ROBERTA HILL, *"Seven Steps to Merger Excellence,"* 2006 , http://www.iveybusinessjournal.com/article.asp?intArticle_ID=778

[xlix] See note xxix, J. P. Chevriere.

[l] See note xxxii, Bill Pursche.

[li] See note xxxii, Bill Pursche.

[lii] Ronald N. Ashkenas, Lawrence J. DeMonaco, and Suzanne C. Francis, "Making the Deal Real:How GE Capital Integrates Acquisitions," *Harvard Business Review* (JANUARY – FEBRUARY 1998) Reprint 98101 http://www.fin.nchu.edu.tw/images/GE%20Capital.pdf

[liii] See note xxix, J. P. Chevriere.

[liv] See note xxxii, Bill Pursche.

[lv] See note xxxiv, Christopher Kummer.

[lvi] See note xxxiv, Christopher Kummer.

[lvii] Booz, Allen & Hamilton, *"Merger Integration: Delivering on the Promise,"* 2001.

[lviii] See note xxix, J. P. Chevriere.

[lix] See note xxix, J. P. Chevriere.

[lx] See note xxix, J. P. Chevriere.

[lxi] Please see Cheveriere, Note I.
[lxii] Ronald N. Ashkenas, Lawrence J. DeMonaco, and Suzanne C. Francis, "Ronald N. Ashkenas, Lawrence J. DeMonaco, and Suzanne C. Francis," *Harvard Business Review* (JANUARY – FEBRUARY 1998) Reprint 98101
http://www.fin.nchu.edu.tw/images/GE%20Capital.pdf

[lxiii] See previous note. Ashkenas et al.

[lxiv] See previous note, Ashkernas, et al.

[lxv] See previous note, Ashkernas et al.

[lxvi] See previous note, Ashkenas et al

[lxvii] See previous note, Ashkenas et al

[lxviii] See note xxxiv, Christopher Kummer.

[lxix] See note xxxiv, Christopher Kummer.

[lxx] See note xxix, J. P. Cheveriere.

[lxxi] See note xxix, J.P. Cheveriere.

[lxxii] See note lxiii,. Ashkenas, et al.

[lxxiii] See note lxiii, Ashkenas, et al.

[lxxiv] See note lxiii, Ashkenas, et al.

[lxxv] See note lxiii, Ashkenas, et al.

[lxxvi] See note xxxiv, Christopher Kummer.

[lxxvii] PricewaterhouseCoopers, *"Post Merger Integration Survey 2009 European results Delivering Deal Value"*, 2009

[lxxviii] See note lxiii . Ashkenas, et al.

[lxxix] See note lxiii. Ashkenas, et al.

[lxxx] Roger Miller, " How Culture Affects Mergers and Acquisitions," , *Industrial Management,* September 1, 2000, http://www.allbusiness.com/human-resources/employee-development/687257-1.html

[lxxxi] Oliver Recklies, "Mergers and Corporate Culture," *Recklies Management Project GmbH*, 2001 § www.themanager.org

[lxxxii] See note lxxx, Roger Miller.

[lxxxiii] See note lxxx, Oliver Recklies.

[lxxxiv] See note lxxxi, Oliver Recklies

[lxxxv] See note lxxx, Roger Miller.

[lxxxvi] See note lxxxi, Oliver Recklies

[lxxxvii] See note lxxxi, Oliver Recklies

[lxxxviii] See note lxiii. Ashkenas, et al.

[lxxxix] See note lxiii. Ashkenas, et al.

[xc] See note lxxx, Oliver Recklies

[xci] See note lxiii Ashkenas, et al,

[xcii] See note lxxx, Oliver Recklies

[xciii] Sharona Peng. " Achieving Successful Cross-Cultural and Management Integration: The Experience of Lenovo and IBM," Masteral Thesis for a Masters in Business, Auckland University of Technology, 2008, http://hdl.handle.net/10292/486 (citations omitted)

[xciv] See note xciii, Sharona Peng.

[xcv] See note xciii, Sharona Peng.

[xcvi] See note xciii, Sharona Peng.

[xcvii] See note xciii, Sharona Peng.

[xcviii] See note xciii Sharona Peng.

[xcix] See note xciii, Sharona Peng.

[c] Steven H. Appelbaum, Jesse Robert Ts and Barbara T. Shapiro, "Cultural Strategies in M & As: Investigating Ten Case Studies,: *Journal of Executive Education* (8) (1) (2009) http://www.appelbaumconsultants.com/articles/2009-10/CulturalStrategies.pdf citing Feldman and Murata, 1991.

[ci] See previous note , Appelbaum, et al.

[cii] See previous note , Appelbaum, et al. citing Bijlisma-Frankema, 2001.

[ciii] See previous note , Appelbaum et al, citing Bijlisma-Frankema, 2001.

[civ] See previous note, Appelbaum et al, citing Eiselle, 1996

[cv] See previous note , Appelbaum et al
[cvi] See previous note , Appelbaum et al, citations omitted.

[cvii] See previous note Appelbaum et al, citations omitted

[cviii] See previous note , Appelbaum et al, citing Cartwright and Cooper, 1993.

[cix] See previous note , Appelbaum et al, Citing Want, 2003.

[cx] See note xxxiv, Christopher Kummer.

[cxi] See note xxxiv, Christopher Kummer.

[cxii] See note xxxiv, Christopher Kummer.

[cxiii] See note xxxiv, Christopher Kummer.

[cxiv] See note xxxiv, Christopher Kummer.

[cxv] See note xxxiv, Christopher Kummer.

[cxvi] See note lxiii . Ashkenas, et al. The story was adapted from their article.

[cxvii] See note lxiii. Ashkenas, et al.

[cxviii] See note lxiii. Ashkenas, et al

[cxix] See note lxiii. Ashkenas, et al

[cxx] See note lxiii. Ashkenas, et al

[cxxi] See note lxiii. Ashkenas, et al

[cxxii] See note lxiii. Ashkenas, et al

[cxxiii] See note lxiii. Ashkenas, et al

56

[cxxiv] See note lxiii. Ashkenas, et al

[cxxv] See note lxiii. Ashkenas, et al

[cxxvi] See note lxiii. Ashkenas, et al

[cxxvii] See note lxiii. Ashkenas, et al

[cxxviii] See note lxiii. Ashkenas, et al

[cxxix] See note lxiii. Ashkenas, et al

[cxxx] See note lxiii. Ashkenas, et al

[cxxxi] See note lxiii. Ashkenas, et al

[cxxxii] See note lxiii. Ashkenas, et al

[cxxxiii] See note lxiii. Ashkenas, et al

[cxxxiv] Alexa Fletcher, Business Transformation Solutions: Avoiding post-merger blues, http://www.manda-institute.org/docs/m&a/bearingpoint_01_avoiding%20post-merger%20blues.pdf

[cxxxv] See previous note Alexa Fletcher.

[cxxxvi] See previous note Alexa Fletcher.

[cxxxvii] See previous note Alexa Fletcher.

[cxxxviii] See previous note Alexa Fletcher.

[cxxxix] Badrtalei, Jeff and Bates, Donald L, "Effect of Organizational Cultures on Mergers and Acquisitions: The Case of DaimlerChrysler" *International Journal of Management, Jun 2007,* http://findarticles.com/p/articles/mi_qa5440/is_200706/ai_n21292857/

[cxl] See previous note Badrtalei et al.

[cxli] See previous note Badrtalei et al

[cxlii] See previous note Badrtalei et al, citations omitted.

[cxliii] See previous note Badrtalei et al, citations omitted.

[cxliv] See previous note Badrtalei et al, citations omitted.

[cxlv] See previous note, Badrtalei et al, citations omitted.

[cxlvi] See note c, , Appelbaum, et al.

[cxlvii] See note xciii, Sharona Peng; "Lenovo Group Ltd. – Company Profile, Information, Business Description, History, Background Information on Lenovo Group Ltd.", http://www.referenceforbusiness.com/history2/52/Lenovo-Group-Ltd.html; Jeffery Brinkhus, Kenneth Keaney, Kathleen McLaughlin, Benjamin Smith, Ziheng Zhu, "Final Paper: Lenovo Group Limited Plus 3 Departure Project " Lenovo Group Limited.

[cxlviii] See previous note, Lenovo Group Ltd. – Company Profile, Information, Business Description, History, Background Information on Lenovo Group Ltd."

[cxlix] See nove xciii, Sharona Peng.

[cl] Official Lenovo website, "Company History," http://www.lenovo.com/lenovo/us/en/history.html

[cli] See note cl, Official Lenovo website, "Company History,"

[clii] See note xciii, Sharona Peng.

[cliii] See note xciii ,, Sharona Peng.

[cliv] John Ackerly and Måns Larsson, "The Emergence of a Global PC Giant: Lenovo's Acquisition of IBM's PC Division, " Final Paper Submitted to Professor Mihir Desai, Cambridge, 2005, http://people.hbs.edu/mdesai/IFM05/AckerlyLarsson.pdf

[clv] "Lenovo and IBM: East Meets West, Big-Time ," http://www.businessweek.com/magazine/content/05_19/b3932113_mz063.htm

[clvi] See note clv "Lenovo and IBM: East Meets West, Big-Time"

[clvii] See note xciii, Sharona Peng.

[clviii] See note xciii, Sharona Peng

[clix] See note xciii, Sharona Peng

[clx] See note xciii, Sharona Peng

[clxi] See note xciii, Sharona Peng

[clxii] See note xciii,Sharona Peng

[clxiii] See note cliv John Ackerly and Måns Larsson

[clxiv] See note clv, "Lenovo and IBM: East Meets West, Big-Time"

[clxv] See note cliv, John Ackerly and Måns Larsson

clxvi See note cliv, John Ackerly and Måns Larsson

clxvii JULIE CHAO, " Lenovo's Corporate Culture a Key Issue as it Absorbs IBM", *World Media Digest*, 12.14.04,
http://www.forbes.com/feeds/general/2004/12/14/generalcoxnews_2004_12_14_eng-coxnews_eng-coxnews_093428_6883557114389138522.html?partner=yahoo&referrer=Cox News Service

clxviii See previous note Julie Chao.

clxix See previous note Julie Chao.

clxx See previous note Julie Chao.

clxxi See previous note Julie Chao.

clxxii See previous note Julie Chao.

clxxiii See previous note Julie Chao.

clxxiv See note xciii, Sharona Peng

clxxv See note xciii, Sharona Peng citing Hofstede, G. H., and Hofstede, G. J. (2005) Cultures and Organizations: Software of the Mind. New York: McGraw-Hill, 2005.

clxxvi See note xciii, Sharona Peng citing Lee, D., J., Pae, J., H. and Wong, Y. H. (2001). "A model of close business relationships in China (Guanxi). "*European Journal of Marketing*, 35, ½, 51-70. And Wong, A., Tjosvold, D., & Yu, Z. (2005). "Organizational partnerships in China: Self-interest, goal interdependence and opportunism." *Journal of Applied Psychology*, 90, 782–791.

clxxvii See note xciii, Sharona Peng

clxxviii See note xciii, Sharona Peng citing Hofstede, G. H. (1984). "Culture's Consequences: International Differences in Work-related Values. Beverly Hills: Sage Publications"; Pun, K. F. (2001). "Cultural influences on total quality management adoption in Chinese enterprises: An empirical study," *Total Quality Management*, 12, 323–342 and Very, P., Lubatkin, M., Calori, R. and Veiga, J. (1997), "Relative Standing and the Performance of Recently Acquired European firms," Strategic *Management Journal*, 18, 8, 593-614.

clxxix See note xciii, Sharona Peng citing Hofstede, G. H. (1984). "Culture's Consequences: International Differences in Work-related Values. Beverly Hills: Sage Publications"

clxxx See note xciii , Sharona Peng citing Hofstede, G. H., and Hofstede, G. J. (2005) Cultures and Organizations: Software of the Mind. New York: McGraw-Hill, 2005.

[clxxxi] See note xciii, Sharona Peng citing Hofstede, G. H., and Hofstede, G. J. (2005) Cultures and Organizations: Software of the Mind. New York: McGraw-Hill, 2005.

[clxxxii] See note xciii, Sharona Peng citing Hofstede, G. H., and Hofstede, G. J. (2005) Cultures and Organizations: Software of the Mind. New York: McGraw-Hill, 2005.

[clxxxiii] See note xciii, Sharona Peng citing Hofstede, G. H., and Hofstede, G. J. (2005) Cultures and Organizations: Software of the Mind. New York: McGraw-Hill, 2005.

[clxxxiv] See note xciii, Sharona Peng citing Hofstede, G. H. (1984).

[clxxxv] See note xciii, Sharona Peng citing Hofstede, G. H., and Hofstede, G. J. (2005)

[clxxxvi] See note xciii, Sharona Peng citing Hofstede, G. H., and Hofstede, G. J. (2005)

[clxxxvii] See note xciii, Sharona Peng citing Hofstede, G. H., and Hofstede, G. J. (2005)

[clxxxviii] See note xciii, Sharona Peng citing Hofstede, G. H., and Hofstede, G. J. (2005)

[clxxxix] See note xciii, Sharona Peng citing Hofstede, G. H., and Hofstede, G. J. (2005)

[cxc] See note xciii, Sharona Peng citing Hofstede, G. H., and Hofstede, G. J. (2005)

[cxci] See note xciii, Sharona Peng citing Hofstede, G. H., and Hofstede, G. J. (2005)

[cxcii] See note xciii, Sharona Peng citing Hofstede, G. H (1990); Laurent, A. (1983). The Cultural Diversity of Western Conceptions of Management. *International Studies of Management Organization,* 13, 1-2, 75-96 and Schneider, S. C. (1988). National versus Corporate Culture: Implication for Human Resources Management. *Human Resource Management,* 27, 1, 231-246.

[cxciii] See note clv, *Lenovo and IBM: East Meets West, Big-Time" and* note xciii, Sharona Peng.

[cxciv] Rick Newman, "Lenovo's Great Leap," October 5, 2007, http://money.usnews.com/money/business-economy/articles/2007/10/05/the-chinese-ibm-computer-merger-shows-signs-of-success.html

[cxcv] See note xciii, Sharona Peng

[cxcvi] See note xciii, Sharona Peng

[cxcvii] See note xciii, Sharona Peng

[cxcviii] See note xciii, Sharona Peng

[cxcix] See note xciii, Sharona Peng

[cc] See note xciii, Sharona Peng

60

[cci] See note xciii, Sharona Peng

[ccii] See note xciii , Sharona Peng

[cciii] See note xciii, Sharona Peng

[cciv] See note xciii, Sharona Peng

[ccv] See note xciii, Sharona Peng

[ccvi] See note xciii , Sharona Peng

[ccvii] See note xciii, Sharona Peng

[ccviii] See note xciii, Sharona Peng

[ccix] See note xciii, Sharona Peng

[ccx] See note xciii, Sharona Peng

[ccxi] See note xciii, Sharona Peng

[ccxii] See note xciii, Sharona Peng

[ccxiii] See note xciii, Sharona Peng

[ccxiv] See note xciii, Sharona Peng

[ccxv] See note cxciv, Rick Newman

[ccxvi] By Wang Xing "Lenovo reboots again for 2010", (China Daily, 2009-01-19 07:45, http://www.chinadaily.com.cn/bizchina/2009-01/19/content_7408277.htm

[ccxvii] See previous note, Wang Xing.

[ccxviii] See previous note, Wang Xing.

[ccxix] See previous note, Wang Xing.

[ccxx] Michael Schuman, " Lenovo's Legend Returns" Time Magazine, May 10, 2010, http://www.time.com/time/magazine/article/0,9171,1986004,00.html

[ccxxi] See previous note, Michael Schuman.

[ccxxii] See previous note, Michael Schuman

[ccxxiii] See previous note, Michael Schuman

[ccxxiv] See previous note, Michael Schuman

[ccxxv] See previous note, Michael Schuman

[ccxxvi] See previous note, Michael Schuman

[ccxxvii] See previous note, Michael Schuman
[ccxxviii] See note cixvii, Julie Chao.

[ccxxix] See note ccxx, Michael Schuman

2977583R00034

Printed in Great Britain
by Amazon.co.uk, Ltd.,
Marston Gate.